ENDORSEMENTS

"*The message of this book is that everyone has a duty to oppose cancel culture which is dividing society and fomenting mistrust. The Gospel's instruction is clear: 'Let each one of you speak truth with his neighbour'.*"

Nick Cater
Executive Director, The Menzies Research Centre

"*The prevalence of cancel culture is a sign that we've devolved from a Western liberal democracy to a woke mob 'democracy' where two Marxist wolves and the conservative lamb vote on what's for lunch. It's high time for the lambs to become lions and fight back. Greg Bondar's book is a great start.*"

George Christensen MP
Federal Member for Dawson (QLD)

"*Cancel Culture, as an Angry Child of White Man's Guilt is rampaging through Western Institutions. And the Church is an Arch-Pariah on its List. The Angry Child seems to disdain the Holy Child it is tossing out with the Church's dirty bathwater. And the Church is near paralysed in the dilemma of what to defend and what to confess. We can do both at the same time for repentance is not weakness and courage is a great virtue. Thank you, Greg, for gathering these courageous voices. May God gather equally courageous readers to know what needs saving and what is better burnt.*"

Rev Charles Newington
Former Chairman, FamilyVoice Australia

"*Whatever your faith, readers of this book will understand what it means to be persecuted and cancelled by the left with its aggressive intolerance of Judeo-Christian values. We know!*"

Dr David Adler
President Australian Jewish Association

SILENCING OF THE LAMBS:

Wokeism and Cancel Culture's Attack on Christianity in Australia

Edited by Greg Bondar

Connor Court Publishing

Published in 2022 by Connor Court Publishing Pty Ltd

Copyright © Greg Bondat as editor 2022.

All rights reserved.

No part of this book may be reproduced or transmitted in any form or by any means, electronic or mechanical, including photo copying, recording or by any information storage and retrieval system, without prior permission in writing from the publisher.

Connor Court Publishing Pty Ltd
PO Box 7257
Redland Bay QLD 4165
sales@connorcourt.com
www.connorcourt.com

ISBN: 9781922815040

Front cover picture: Josefa de Óbidos: The Sacrificial Lamb, 1670?, wikipedia commons.

Printed in Australia

CONTENTS

	Foreword	*Kevin Andrews*	7
1	Editorial Commentary: Religion, Wokeism and Cancel Culture – Christianity Under Threat	*Greg Bondar*	11
2	Christianity, Cancel Culture, Tyranny, and History	*Bill Muehlenberg*	17
3	Moral Law and Anti-Discrimination Law	*Peter Barnes*	25
4	The Church is Under Attack	*Judy Russell*	37
5	Woke-ism its Origins and its Effect on the Christian Church	*Ettienne McClintock*	43
6	Understanding the Cause of the Attack on Christianity	*Bernard Gaynor*	55
7	The Devil is Always in the Detail	*Fred Nile*	63
8	Where to from Here?	*Lyle Shelton*	75
9	"The Time for Alibis and Excuses Has Expired" - Religious Freedoms and Parental Rights in the Age of Cancel Culture	*Mark Latham*	93
10	Living Under a New Paradigm	*Hector J. Ramirez Martinez*	111
11	How Not to Respond to Cancel Culture?	*Akos Balogh*	117

Foreword

The notion that religious freedom does not require any further legal protection because Australians are a tolerant, easy-going people is overly sanguine. Hence, a bishop is dragged before a tribunal for simply expounding Catholic beliefs. A company retreats after a twitter storm because it was associated with a respectful debate between two Members of Parliament about same-sex marriage. Activists hound a business executive to resign from the board of a Christian education institution. A sports star is harangued for expressing the belief that marriage is between and a man and a woman. A university is pressured about an academic who supports a Christian foundation. The latter was argued in the name of diversity – a diversity that tolerates only one view!

The notion of toleration has been turned on its head. A new liberal view was espoused by John Locke in his 1689 Letter Concerning Toleration. In it, Locke sought to distinguish the business of civil government from that of religion. Written at a time when controversy surrounded the idea that Catholics should be able to practice their religion in Protestant England, or Jews or Muslims enjoy religious freedom in a Christian nation, Locke argued that the State and the Church had separate functions. He sought to find a way that people of different religious beliefs could live together.

As Jonathan Sacks has written, toleration "aims not so much at truth but at peace. It is a political necessity not a religious imperative, and it arises when people have lived through the alternative: the war of all against all."

Beginning with the libertarian revolution of the 1960s, the notion of a common public morality has been challenged and undermined. Within half a century the political notion that the law should not intrude into areas of private behaviour has been transformed into the moral assertion that a person now has the 'right' to do anything not precluded by law.

The political judgment about the boundaries of the law is now translated into a moral judgment about rights. What one was 'permitted' to do now becomes what one has the 'right' to do. And having asserted a 'right, many insist that it should be protected by the law! Hence Locke's political toleration has been combined with the new moral relativism. As Sacks cautions, when political liberalism is combined with moral relativism it reconnects morality and politics, the very thing liberalism was supposed to avoid.

A moral judgment that liberalism allowed a person to express in the realm of faith and religion – for example about religious belief, including the alleged beliefs, customs, or practices of other religions - is now swept into the political realm. In morally relative politics, a 'right' to do something must be protected as a new human right. Not only is the activity now a 'right,' but the persons involved are right (or at least as right as anyone else). To say otherwise is intolerant. Such intolerance is discriminatory and should be punished. How the wheel has turned in three centuries!

One of the great achievements of the political liberalism of the 17th and 18th centuries was the idea that the individual is the foundation of the polity. The law treated individuals as its basis. This notion was foundational to liberal democracy. Hence in the spirit of this development, the 1776 United States Declaration of

Independence boldly asserted that: "All men are created equal; that they are endowed by their creator with certain unalienable rights; that among these are life, liberty, and the pursuit of happiness; that to secure these rights, governments are instituted among men, deriving their just powers from the consent of the governed."

Under this formulation, it is the individual who possesses political rights and whose consent legitimates government. It was a rejection of the idea that rights subsisted in classes of people, whether determined by birth, hierarchy, or membership of a particular group. It is central to the liberal democratic experiment.

Increasingly however, 'rights' are now being asserted on behalf of groups. A claim is made for example, that the expression of a moral judgment about the beliefs, statements or actions of another group should be unlawful because it is offensive to members of the group; or that it is likely to cause ridicule or contempt towards a member of that group.

Whereas the laws of defamation protect the individual against libel and slander, it is now claimed that moral judgments about a group should be unlawful and punishable. This is a significant shift.

The law of defamation seeks to protect an individual's reputation by providing a civil action against a person who has 'caused hatred, ridicule or contempt' to employ the standard formulation. Western society has traditionally drawn a distinction between offence and defamation. Many unpleasant, offensive things are said in a liberal society like Australia, but they do not constitute defamation.

Freedom of religion includes the freedom "to profess and by argument to maintain, their opinions in matters of religion," to quote Thomas Jefferson's famous formulation. That means in the public square, not just the synagogue, temple or church as covered in the International Covenant on Civil and Political Rights.

These trends are exacerbated in Australia because discrimination on various grounds other than religion is protected by law. Consequently, the imbalance between competing rights and the lack of an appropriate way to resolve the ensuing conflicts is the greatest challenge to freedom of religion in Australia. To quote from the Foreword to the Parliamentary Report on Religious Freedom: "This is most apparent with the advent of non-discrimination laws which do not allow for differentiation of treatment by religious individuals and organisations. It is also manifested in a decreasing threshold for when religious freedom may be limited. For example, the Victorian Charter of Rights and Responsibilities allows 'reasonably necessary' limitations while the ACT Human Rights Act has the even lower threshold of 'reasonable' limitations, compared to the International Covenant's requirement that limitations be 'necessary.' While religious exemptions within non-discrimination laws provide some protection, these place religious freedom in a vulnerable position with respect to the right to non-discrimination, and do not acknowledge the fundamental position that freedom of religion has in international human rights law."

Once freedom of speech is compromised, freedom of religion will not be far behind. And when both are compromised, freedom itself will have been lost.

Hon. Kevin Andrews MP
Australian Federal Parliament

1

Religion, Wokeism, and Cancel Culture – Christianity Under Threat

Greg Bondar – Editor

"To learn who rules over you, find out whom you are not allowed to criticise" - *Voltaire*

If you think woke culture or 'wokeism' with its attendant cancel culture, is not going to bother Christians, the Church, Christianity, or Christ himself, you should think again. "Woke" people often consider themselves or at least those they purport to represent, victims. Consequently, they seem to be offended by everything.

Alternatively, wokeism has developed its view of reality with its own set of values and narratives. From the ashes of secular humanism, a new civil religion rises. Wokeism offers everything that secularism failed to provide and has quickly filled the God-shaped hole in our culture.

What is so nefarious about wokeism is that it regularly plays on people's better motivations such as compassion and a desire for justice. Most people have a genuine desire to see the lives of others improve, and many Christians have engaged with these ideas as if they are congruent with the teachings of Christ. Wokeism is incompatible with the biblical worldview, differing in several keyways. Essentially, it attributes intrinsic guilt or innocence to the individual based on their group identity, regardless of individual actions. Proverbs 17:15. acquitting the guilty and condemning the innocent— the Lord detests them both.

The general societal view is that wokeism is an oppressive mind-virus which thrives on ridicule, humiliation, persistent denigration and now violence *a la* the Black Lives Matter riots.

Historically, wokeism was a Marxist inspired movement that started off with well-intentioned people that wanted to stop racism and social injustice. It has now morphed into a cult that seeks to silence all of those that disagree. The phrase "I disapprove of what you say, but I will defend to the death your right to say it" has lost all meaning.

Wokeism demands equity not equality. It seeks to destroy all norms, to redefine words, and destroy objective science to create a Marxist Utopia. Instead of reducing racism, this new anti-racism is just racism by a different name.

Wokeism is a full-on attack on Western civilisation. It aims to rewrite history to confuse and inspire the destruction of the West. This virus is infecting every part of society. From children's schools, books, health, media, military, entertainment, church and even to Government itself. It is everywhere and is now threatening to end freedom of speech and thought as we knew it. It has become impossible to speak out without fear of career-death and possible physical harm. One only has to look at celebrities and identities such as J.K. Rowling, Piers Morgan, Enid Blyton, and corporate big names that changed to avoid being cancelled including McDonald's, Lego, Monopoly, Washington Redskins, Barbie doll, and Australia's *Coon* cheese manufacturer which has been forced change its name to 'Cheer' after some 90 years of trading as Coon cheese.

Likewise, there are scores of victims of cancel culture. Simply put, cancel culture is the idea of taking away support for an individual, their career, popularity and/or fame because of something they have said or done that is considered unacceptable. To be "cancelled" is effectively to be boycotted, with the intent that the person will be ostracised and no longer benefit financially, personally, or professionally from their elevated position.

Over the last few years, there has been a dramatic increase in violence against those that support freedom of speech. Those that believe in wokeism justify all their actions by saying everyone they do not like are Nazis. These people share one thing in common. They hate their own country and regardless of their race, they blame 'Western Culture' and white people for most of their problems, and society's problems.

This book records what the mainstream media wants to ignore. It is ammunition in the 'Culture War.'

The theme of the book aims to address the issues the broader 'Church' (Christianity) is currently facing in Australia and overseas and how it is being overrun by wokeism and cancel culture with traditional Christian doctrine and values being undermined, attacked, challenged, amended, and/or ignored on such issues as abortion, Same Sex Marriage, gender fluidity, ordination of gay clergy, new rainbow churches, fake Christianity, big tech censoring, anti-Christian government legislation not to mention divisions within the church itself over vaccinations, euthanasia, and abortion alike.

Christianity is the antithesis of 'wokeness' and they are indeed polar opposites. The 'social justice movement' is hijacking the Gospel, has already highjacked the true meaning of the 'rainbow,' has demeaned the meaning of male and female, undermined the history of our western civilisation, ignored the value of life and now it wants society to bow down to the alter of wokeism and cancel culture.

Many theologians offered concrete guidance on the role we all can play in fighting injustice while at the same time rejecting woke utopianism in our churches, and in broader institutions as well.

In doing research for book, I compiled a list of secular voices speaking out against cancel culture and wokeism. The contributors are not just Christian conservatives speaking up but people with vastly different worldviews and convictions speaking up as well – from politicians to pastors.

Cancel culture is like a forest fire in constant need of fuel. Functioning subjectively, full of prejudice, no moral code simply good old search and destroy. The deserving and the undeserving alike are all targets. Even for the staunchest conservative, there is evidence after evidence that 'political correctness' has grown to become the unhappiest religion in the world.

Christian conservatives are used to criticism. Criticism is kosher in the work that we do. Criticism is great. What cancel culture is about is not criticism. It is about punishment. It is about making a person radioactive - toxic. It is about taking away their job, self-respect and indeed their dignity.

There appears to be a paradigm shift with so many from the left and the right pushing back. Some commentators have compared cancel culture to 'social murder.'

We must not continue to allow our Judaeo-Christian heritage to be highjacked. The fact is that this is Australia, and our nation was built on fundamental freedoms, including the freedom of speech. And when such a fundamental freedom gets threatened, you can be assured that there will be a pushback – and not just from Christian conservatives concerned about their religious liberties, but from people like the former British Prime Minister Tony Blair whom no one would brand a Christian conservative.

Blair has called for common-sense in the debates on biological sex, trans rights and free speech. In a wide-ranging interview with *The Times* Magazine, Sir Tony highlighted voter resistance to radical transgender ideology and criticised the practice of no-platforming in academia. Blair said: "It's ridiculous saying you can't go and talk at a university if you say something I might not agree with. You have to come to common-sense positions on these things and hold firm to them."

On issues such as the conflict between women's rights and transgenderism, Blair said: "The polls might say voters don't care but if you dig a little deeper, what they are really saying is we don't like all this stuff that is being shoved at us." Equal rights do not mean you cannot use the phrase 'pregnant woman.' Women do not want a situation where they cannot talk about being women.

My hope for the Church in a rapidly changing world is that we would become a collaborative Church. I think of collaboration in layers of concentric circles, each circle smaller and more focused than the previous one. In the 1950s, one's identity was closely tied to religion. Parents would be more concerned if their child wanted to marry someone of a different faith than a different political party. Today the opposite is true. As Christians, our primary identity should be who we are in Christ not what trendy wokeism is the flavour of the month.

Wokeism and cancel culture is much bigger than the world of religion. This is about pushing back against the 'thought police,' the morally bankrupt, the self-appointed gurus of ethics. This book is about resisting intellectual tyranny the inaptly named progressive elites. It is about saying 'no' to, what has become the catch phrase, the 'looney-left' found in the media, government, Big Tech, education, and the entertainment industry and indeed the secular society at large.

Is cancel culture eroding our freedoms? Absolutely. Dr Kameel Majdali from 'Understand the Times' believes it is. There is something wrong in a society that tells everyone to be offended by everything. That tells people to be ashamed of their whiteness. That tells them they would somehow be less offensive if they were 'less white.'

Australia needs to reclaim its heritage, its language, its sexuality, its Judeo-Christian principles and say goodbye to wokeism in government, the military, education, media, sport, public debate and finally the gratuitous wokesim practiced by the corporate sector.

To Reclaim Australia from the ravages of wokeism and cancel culture, we need to cross the Rubicon. Enough is enough. It's time to break people out of the postmodernist thought prison and stop the woke movement. It's time to reclaim Australia's Judeo-Christian heritage.

Let the reclamation begin! *alea iacta est*

***

Greg Bondar is a Christian, an Apologist, Chaplain, Lay Preacher and NSW/ACT State Director of FamilyVoice Australia. He was a former senior adviser in the first term of the John Howard government.

2

Christianity, Cancel Culture, Tyranny, and History

Bill Muehlenberg

In April of 2021 there was a news item about enraged parents who had discovered that their boys at a Melbourne secondary school had been labelled as "oppressors" for being, male, white and Christian. Their crime was simply to exist and to fall afoul of the leftist lynch mob.

History and current events tell us the same story: There is a war on Christianity, and the endgame of cancel culture is the cancellation of it. Clearly this is where things have always been heading. Cancel culture, identity politics, the woke brigade, and political correctness are all aiming their big guns at the one last obstacle standing in their way of complete control.

And I happen to know a little bit about what it is like to be cancelled simply for having a point of view that differs from the secular left narrative. Over the years for example I have had various stints in the Facebook Gulag for stating my Christian and conservative opinions on some of the major topics of the day. But in May they decided that I was a repeat offender – an unrepentant recidivist – and therefore I must be punished with a permanent ban.

I was never informed of my actual crimes or sins – I was simply cancelled. There are countless others just like me of course who have met the same fate. Indeed, examples of cancel culture seem to be never ending. As Rowan Atkinson recently said: "The problem we have online is that an algorithm decides what we want to see, which ends up creating a simplistic, binary view of society. It becomes a case of either you're with us or against us. And if you're against us, you deserve to be 'cancelled.' It's important that we're exposed to a wide spectrum of opinion, but what we have now is the digital equivalent of the medieval mob roaming the streets looking for someone to burn. So, it is scary for anyone who's a victim of that mob and it fills me with fear about the future."

But it is not just 'Mr Bean' who is quite concerned about this matter – numerous voices are now speaking out about it, and various books from overseas have already appeared on the topic, including:

Alan Dershowitz, *Cancel Culture* (Hot Books, 2020).

Ben Shapiro, *The Authoritarian Moment: How the Left Weaponized America's Institutions Against Dissent* (Broadside Books, 2021).

Michael Knowles, *Speechless: Controlling Words, Controlling Minds* (Regnery, 2021).

Stephen Strang, *God, and Cancel Culture: Standing Strong for the Truth* (Frontline, 2021).

Michael Brown, *The Silencing of the Lambs: The Ominous Rise of Cancel Culture and How We Can Overcome It (*due out March 2022).

Any serious student of history will not be surprised by this. They will know full well the obvious: all tyrannical regimes have relied on the three Cs of censorship, control, and cancellation. That is how they maintain power and keep the masses suppressed and fully compliant. As Strang puts it:

"Cancel Culture really isn't new. Censorship, propaganda, and coercion have always been tools of the powerful throughout history, going by different names in each generation and under each new, intolerant regime. The purpose is always to silence opponents and control society by dominance and intimidation."

One of the most obvious examples of cancel culture in the recent past concerns the book burnings done in Nazi Germany. For example, on May10/11, 1933, at the instigation and direction of the State, thousands of students in every university town in Germany gathered large piles of books and set them alight.

All up, some 25,000 volumes of "un-German" books were destroyed. And all this received widespread and positive newspaper and radio coverage. This of course was just one aspect of German state censorship and control of the culture that was taking place during the time.

Lest people think this is the stuff of 'ancient' history, consider a much more recent book burning that took place in Canada. In September of this year "it was reported in Canadian media that in 2019 a 'flame purification ceremony' was held by the French language school board Conseil scolaire catholique Providence, which oversees elementary and secondary schools in southwestern Ontario."

Almost 5000 books were pulled from library shelves, and many were burned: "In total, more than 4700 books were removed from library shelves at 30 schools across the school board, and they have since been destroyed or are in the process of being recycled. Books were burned if they had elements of racism, discrimination and stereotypes."[1]

Scary stuff indeed. How reminiscent of what took place in the 1930s. And of course, the Nazis were not just destroying books and suppressing ideas – they were seeking to eliminate entire groups of people. We need to recall the words of the German Jewish poet Heinrich Heine (1797-1856): "Where they burn books, they will also ultimately burn people." To totally control a people and their ideas, killing the recalcitrant is usually what is resorted to.

The French Revolution was another obvious example of hardcore cancel culture in action. The church was a major target, and an all-out war was declared against it. As one writer explains in rather gory detail: "In September 1792, an event known as the September Massacres claimed the lives of 1200 to 1400 people in less than four days when revolutionary mobs stormed the Paris jails and murdered men, women, and children by hacking them to pieces or bashing their skulls in. Of those killed, 233 were Catholic priests that refused the oath demanded of them in the "Civil Constitution of the Clergy," which placed the Church under state control.

"Spurred on by rebellions in the countryside, the revolutionaries by 1793 would jettison the principles laid out in the "Declaration of the Rights of Man" with the institution of a secret police that would monitor citizen activity and arrest anyone they deemed unfriendly to the revolution. Informants were stationed everywhere, and people could be carted off to the guillotine for so much as addressing people in the old-fashioned "Monsieur" and "Madame" instead of the state sanctioned "citoyen" (citizen). Even back in 1793, leftists were butchering common terms.

"Robespierre and the Jacobins regarded the Catholic Church and Christianity in general as little more than a cloying reminder of France's monarchical and superstitious past. To fully sever from it, they launched an era of dechristianization that included the state's confiscation of Church property, the destruction of Christian icons, and instituting of bizarre civic cults, including the Cult of Reason and the Cult of the Supreme Being. All priests and clergymen that did not swear the oath mandated in the "Civil Constitution" were liable to execution on site.

"None felt this dechristianization quite so harshly as the peasants in the coastal region of the Vendée, who became subject to what some historians have classified as the first modern genocide, with the current death toll 170,000."[2]

Many others have discussed this of course. In her book on leftist mob rage, *Demonic*, Ann Coulter wrote about the Revolutionaries' zeal to cancel Christianity. She reminds us that anything associated with the old order was targeted by the mobs, but anything having to do with the church was especially focused on. Priests, nuns, and lay people were massacred in large numbers, while churches were destroyed and one sacrilege after another was carried out. Some of the gruesome descriptions of what the mobs did to ordinary men, women and children are almost too hard to stomach. Rape, torture, mutilation, and hideous forms of killing were the norm. If one had to illustrate the actions of the demonic, surely this was it. It seemed there were not enough guillotines to keep up with all the carnage and slaughter. And all the while the crowds were cheering this on. The Jacobin program of "de-Christianisation" was especially ferocious and repellent. Indeed, "the word *'vandalisme'* had to be invented to describe" their actions as they desecrated churches, looted Christian properties, and destroyed sacred art. The revolutionaries sought to "completely destroy Christianity and replace it with a religion of the state". Anything associated with Christianity was open to attack. Citizens were even forced to drop their Christian names. A new Revolutionary Calendar was established, with the months renamed, and even clocks were redesigned in decimal time.

Sadly, the same anti-Christian cancel culture still exists today. In places like North Korea and Communist China we see this being played out on an epic scale. And in many Muslim-majority nations we see the same thing occurring. Consider just one recent example of what we find happening in China: "Religious freedom is barely even a concept in communist China, and now it's under fresh assault from the anti-Christian regime. Chinese American Pastor Bob Fu of the group China Aid, which provides legal aid to Christians in the People's Republic, recently tweeted, "New Cultural Revolution" starts in #CCPChina this notice to students in a 1st Grade class demanding all parents and teachers to hunt all "religious books, antagonistic books & overseas books including books & videos that are copied/duplicated &translated. Everyone is mandated!"[3]

We expect this to occur with a passion in such Christophobic countries. What is so shocking is to find the democratic free West heading down the same path. Over the years I have documented countless examples of this. And other chapters in this book offer plenty of cases of cancel culture in full swing in the West – especially targeting Christians and Christianity.

But let me present just one recent alarming case of cancel culture in action. Western universities used to be known as places of free thought and open inquiry. Staff and students were once free to explore various ideas and discuss even the most controversial topics. Not any more it seems. What happened at Oxford university is a case in point: "One of Oxford University's constituent colleges, Worcester College, has apologized for allowing an Evangelical campaign group, Christian Concern, to book its facilities for a residential event during the summer break. The fact that the event had taken place at all only became known to the college's radicalized students when one of them found a flyer from the event lying around. Since the students were not in residence at the time, they missed the chance to be upset by hearing any of the talks or discussions or traumatized by meeting any of the attendees. They had to make do with their distress at the fact that the college's hallowed meeting rooms and corridors had felt the presence of a wider range of views than has become usual. Worcester College realized too late its mistake, issuing a statement: "We deeply regret the distress caused to students, staff and other members of the college community by the presence of the Wilberforce Academy conference."[4]

I conclude with a few quotes from a great selection of essays assembled in *Cancel Culture* (Wilkinson, 2021). One of the authors, human rights lawyer John Steenhof, looks at various cases that have made the headlines in Australia of late, including sports star Israel Folau, Tasmanian Archbishop Julian Porteous, Christian medical doctor Jereth Kok, and various "conversion therapy" laws. All these examples have to do with a crackdown on religious freedom.

Says Steenhof: "Freedom of religion is particularly vulnerable to cancel culture that uses lawfare – the process of attempting to coerce or punish a person's actions through litigation. While religious freedom is widely recognised in international law, it has little express protection in Australian law."

The direct threat of cancel culture on religious thought, conviction and expression is a very real problem indeed. The result of all this is "a society of mandated opinions, excoriated religion and tepid groupthink." A culture such as this cannot last long unless there is a resolute push-back by a concerned citizenry.

And historian Stephen Chavura's chapter looks at the way forward. He reminds us that the only speech now tolerated "is that which conforms to a leftist social agenda." The stifling of free speech and the cancellation of alternate points of view is the bitter fruit of many decades of leftist militancy.

He also looks at various examples of this, and then says: "At the end of the day cancel culture thrives on timidity. Even though people in general are not as passionate about free speech as we might hope, the claims of cancel culture regarding others' rights to speak freely and not have their livelihood and reputations destroyed by virtual mobs are almost certainly not as widely shared in society as they would like to think."

Yes, quite right. The mobs always exploit the fear and cowardice of the people. It is only when we take a courageous stance that we can resist this insidious cancel culture and anti-Christian bigotry. As Billy Graham once put it, "Courage is contagious. When a brave man takes a stand, the spines of others are often stiffened."

Courage and uncompromising Christian conviction are certainly the need of the hour.

References

1. Mitchell Van Homrigh, Canadian schools under fire for 'reconciliation' book burning, September 13, 2021. News.com.au

2. Paul Bois, I'm a French Catholic; I'd Rather Eat Costco Baguettes Than Celebrate 'Bastille Day', July 15, 2017. DailyWire.com.

3. Steve Warren, Crackdown: China Orders Citizens to 'Hunt Down' All Books with Religion, State 'Church' Sings Pro-Communist Song, June 28, 2021. CBN News (Online).

4. Joseph Shaw, Oxford college caves to woke mob, apologizes for letting Christians use campus, September 28, 2021. Lifesitenews.com

Bill Muehlenberg is social and Christian commentator with his blog CultureWatch

3

Moral Law and Anti-Discrimination Law

Rev Dr Peter Barnes

The reconciliation of law and freedom has always been a minefield, but since the onset of anti-discrimination laws and an anti-discrimination cultural mentality, it has become a minefield in a quagmire. Many, perhaps most, Western Christians in the present climate have tended to argue something along the lines of: (a) Fairness and freedom are good values.

(b) Anti-discrimination laws protect people from unfair treatment.

(c) Therefore, a law protecting religious people from discrimination is only fair and just.[1]

The sentiments may be soothing, but the reality may bring little comfort.

The elites of society have been able to gain credence for the view that all moral values are relative, and especially that there is no such thing as sexual ethics. Everything, including one's gender, is a matter of personal choice. The results are before us: millions of abortions in the West each year; just about any liaison with anything is probably legal, and unlikely to be prosecuted if it is not; and a widespread breakdown in family life. Yet we are reluctant to face the fact that something is radically wrong.

The Balance of Freedom and Law

Francis Schaeffer stated cogently: 'What the Reformation's return to biblical teaching gave society was the opportunity for tremendous freedom, but without chaos. That is, an individual had freedom because there was a consensus based upon the absolutes given in the Bible, and therefore real values within which to have freedom, without these freedoms leading to chaos.'[2] The Bible sees the importance of lawful order and rightful freedom.

The atheistic philosopher, A. C. Grayling, has gone on the attack to assert that the public domain needs to be completely secularised: 'Mankind's future needs the public domain to be a neutral territory where all can meet, without prejudice, as humans and equals; and that requires the wholesale privatisation of superstition.'[3] And he cannot see the irony. Liberalism, left to its own devices, manages only to eat itself up.

The New Testament sees the basic role of the civil authorities in terms of administering justice, of curbing what is evil and promoting what is good (e.g., Rom.13:1-7; 1 Peter 2:13-17). Tensions - even inconsistencies - can be seen in Christian thinking on these issues down through the ages, but there is good reason to take Calvin very seriously: 'No polity can be successfully established unless piety is its first cause.'[4]

Increasingly, society is being held together - if it is being held together - by a shared commitment to what Juvenal called 'bread and circuses'. So, we all must rally around sporting heroes or celebrities of one kind or another. Without Christ, there is no point of integration and no unifying factor; it all falls apart.

Two Kinds of Law

Freedom requires virtue if it is not to be mob rule, and virtue requires an authority outside the rule of Hollywood, academia, and the internet. God's Law sustains human law. In fact, it is written on the hearts of all humanity, and testified to by our consciences (Rom.2:12-16).

The Westminster Confession delineates three parts to God's law: moral law, ceremonial laws, and judicial laws (WCF, XIX). But for our purposes we need to separate out two kinds of biblical law. First, there is what we might call 'moral law' which consists of the commandments which forbid idolatry, murder, sexual immorality, stealing, and other sins (see Exodus 20:1-17).

Then there is what we might call 'discrimination law' where, for example, God forbids partiality, or what in modern parlance is more likely to be referred to as 'discrimination'. In the Old Testament, God declared to Israel: 'You shall do no injustice in court. You shall not be partial to the poor or defer to the great, but in righteousness shall you judge your neighbour' (Lev.19:15; see too Ex.23:3, 6, 9;). Furthermore, 'Cursed be anyone who perverts the justice due to the sojourner, the fatherless, and the widow. And all the people shall say, "Amen"' (Deuteronomy 27:19; see too Deut. 10:17; 2 Chron.19:7; Job 34:9).

The New Testament essentially repeats the moral commandments (e.g., Rom.13:8-10) and the command to show no partiality (James 2:9), for God himself shows no partiality (Acts 10:34; Romans 2:11; 1 Peter 1:17). It might seem as though the 'no partiality' approach of the Bible is rather like the 'no discrimination' approach in modern law, but this is not so.

In the biblical approach, discrimination law feeds off moral law. To give one obvious example, the Bible forbids homosexual acts as unnatural offences against primary moral law (Lev.18:22).

Therefore, the prohibition against showing partiality cannot be interpreted in a way that protects sexual immorality. Toleration within biblical boundaries is laudable (Rom.14:1, 10; 15:1); outside those boundaries it to be rejected (2 Cor.11:4; Rev.2:20). What happens in modern law - and in the popular perception of it - is that discrimination law has increasingly taken on primary moral characteristics, even an absolutist tone. To discriminate against someone becomes an offence against the first and great - and even only! - commandment.

The Moral Law, Relativism and Cultural Marxism

Relativism has been with us since the Fall. In the dark days of the Judges everyone did what was right in his own eyes (Judges 21:25) - a frame of mind not unknown today. In the 1980s, Allan Bloom commented on the beliefs of American college students: "There is one thing a professor can be absolutely certain of: almost every student entering the university believes, or says he believes, that truth is relative ... The relativity of truth is not a theoretical insight but a moral postulate, the condition of a free society, or so they see it ... Relativism is necessary to openness, and this is the virtue, the only virtue, which all primary education for more than fifty years has dedicated itself to inculcating."[5]

It is not just an American phenomenon; it is a Western malaise. And it has not resulted in an expansion of minds, but a constriction.

One of the more remarkable conversions to Christ in recent times is that of Rosaria Champagne Butterfield, who was formerly a lesbian English Professor. She has recorded what she had written concerning her Women's Studies 101 syllabus: "NB: Students are expected to write all papers and examination essay questions from a feminist worldview or critical perspective. In Spanish class you speak and think in Spanish. In Women's Studies you speak and think in feminist paradigms. Examination essay questions written from critical perspectives outside of feminism will receive an automatic grade of F. Papers written from critical perspectives outside of feminism will be allowed one revision. Any student who is unable to write and think from a feminist critical perspective or worldview with a clear conscience should drop the class now."[6]

There are few things more totalitarian than a fashionable way of thinking. G. K. Chesterton saw it coming: 'We are on the road to producing a race of men too mentally modest to believe in the multiplication table.'[7] The wider issue is that relativism does not lead to arguments between competing truth claims, but to the conclusion that truth claims have no meaning.

Francis Schaeffer wrote back in 1984 of 'the pressure of an all-pervasive culture built upon relativism and relativistic thinking.'[8] Moral relativism is self-refuting. It is like saying 'There are absolutely no absolutes' or 'the law of contradiction is false' or 'everything I say is a lie'. That does not bother the moral relativists. They take the moral high ground, and think they are saving the world from fascism, but they are easily caught out, in terms of logic at least.

In the 1950s Herbert Marcuse discovered a new set of victims: dark-skinned people, women, and homosexuals. These are portrayed, most unconvincingly as homogenous groups, whom Noel Weeks has labelled 'Marx's stepchildren'. All virtue belongs with the alleged victims, and all evil is attributed to the alleged oppressors.[9] It is not altogether unusual for cures to kill more than the disease, and for revolutionaries to excel at repression. Classical freedom-focused liberalism has degenerated into a modern rights-based liberalism,[10] which is more adversarial, ill-defined, and dependent on state support. Slogans have replaced thought, in the savagely ironic words of François Thom, in order 'to protect ideology from the malicious attacks of real things.'[11] Never has critical thinking been held in such high esteem and never has it been so woefully practised. Western education systems promote critiques before there is a capacity to critique.

The Connection between Decadence and Brutality

Permissiveness has led to authoritarianism. The Canaanite culture in the Old Testament was both debased and brutal (see Lev.18). That fits reality. In Dostoyevsky's The Devils Peter Verkhovensky perceives the link between authoritarianism and promiscuity. He declares that 'one or two generations of vice are essential now.'[12] With seared consciences, people were prepared to commit almost any act of barbarity. Often the dictatorship of Josef Stalin is portrayed as a betrayal of the revolution - as in George Orwell's Animal Farm, for example. Stalin fulfilled the revolution. From the beginning, he was an amoral thug who, for example, simply robbed banks when the Bolsheviks were short of funds.[13]

Nazi Germany is not to be interpreted as conservative decency gone to seed, but as an outworking of human decadence. The head of the SA (the brown-shirted storm troopers) was Ernst Röhm (1887-1934), who duly organised assassinations and street fights in favour of the National Socialists.[14] Throughout the 1920s he was the only Nazi leader to be allowed to address Hitler with the familiar 'Du'. He was thoroughly educated, well-mannered, and a more than capable pianist, yet his decadent lifestyle saw him contract gonorrhoea three times.[15] By 1924 he had entered the Reichstag, albeit briefly, as a member of the misnamed National Socialist Freedom Party, as well as becoming head of the SA. At the same time, he consciously adopted a homosexual identity and unapologetic lifestyle.[16]

Berlin in the 1920s was renowned for its open homosexual rights movement, and Röhm wrote of it: 'The bath house there is however still in my view the peak of all human happiness.'[17] He also knew the language of righteousness, and mocked what he labelled hypocrisy and prudery, campaigning strongly for the League of Human Rights. At the same time, he paid under-age sexual partners.[18] The degenerate and the brutal belong together.

What Happens when Moral Law and Discrimination Law are Disconnected?

Sexuality is now defined in terms of being, not behaviour, and so is regarded as protected 'truth'. Over past decades Western governments have virtually all passed Anti-Discrimination Acts which have usually allowed exemptions for sexuality for churches, Christian schools, and perhaps other religious organisations. Logically, that will not last; it has aroused resentment against religious bodies; and it is crumbling before our eyes. This is wonderful news for the unelected lawyers and judges who sit on anti-discrimination boards. As Charles Dickens commented in Bleak House: 'The one great principle of the English law is, to make business for itself.'[19] The philosophy creates the office, and the office then perpetuates the philosophy. Anti-Discrimination Boards will only ever achieve justice in bits and pieces, on odd occasions. Law will exist without a coherent rationale and foundation, and when two 'freedoms' collide, the result will be whatever passes for justice in the eye of the beholder.

The homosexual activist, Rodney Croome, has sounded the alarm against allowing a baker to refuse an order for a gay wedding cake: 'the next step is a sign in the window saying, "No

Gays", and the step after that a sign that says, "No Muslims" or "No Blacks".[20] It has been a remarkably successful marketing strategy which identifies disparate concepts: skin colour (over which none of us has any control) and beliefs (e.g., Islam, which one can believe or disbelieve) and sexual behaviour (which we may or may not practise).

Logically, if anti-discrimination laws are good, there ought to be no exemptions. However, where there is no clear concept of moral law, tolerance takes its place, and finding itself in a moral vacuum, then becomes intolerant. Moving inexorably on, those who previously argued for toleration have become the winners and constitute a new establishment. We dwell amid a culture of moral outrage and indignation, and what was previously regarded as sinful now demands affirmation.

Modern laws are trying to do too much. Thomas Watson stated: 'Man's law binds the hands only, God's law binds the heart.'[21] We are now witnessing civil law which aims at the heart and deals with so-called hate speech and attitudes. Homosexuality must be more than tolerated; it must be pandered to and approved. It seems George Orwell hit the mark near the end of Nineteen Eighty-Four where Winston is told: 'You must love Big Brother. It is not enough to obey him: you must love him.'[22]

Conclusion

When asked in 1933 why he did not join the German Christians to work against them from within, Dietrich Bonhoeffer replied that he could not: 'If you board the wrong train, it is no use running along the corridor in the opposite direction.'[23] We are trying to find religious freedoms and a fair order within a framework of anti-discrimination legislation. It will only deliver state-subsidised perversion and an adversarial structure for civil interactions. We are on the wrong train.

Freedom and order need to be reconciled, as in the words of the Psalmist: 'And I will walk at liberty, for I seek Your precepts' (Ps.119:45). Civil law requires a moral basis, and in the long term, only God's law can provide that basis. This is repudiated in Hebert Marcuse's vision of 1965: 'the exercise of civil rights by those who don't have them presupposes the withdrawal of civil rights from those who prevent their exercise'.[24]

If societies become ungodly and corrupt, laws will not transform them. They will, instead, become part of the wider problem. It has become obvious what should have been quite clear at the beginning:

(a) the modern approach to law is lawyer-driven, adversarial, and oppressive;

(b) law can never deliver freedoms, but it has the potential to take them away;

(c) there is such a thing as common grace, but it easily fractures;

(d) Christianity provides the only realistic basis for balancing freedom and law;

(e) the state of the Church is more crucial than the state of the wider society (Gen.18:16-33; Matt. 5:14-16; 1 Peter 4:17).

All things hold together in Christ, and only in Christ (Col.1:17). The quest for perfectionism without a humble awareness of our sin has led to delusion and coercion. Let us take heart from what Phillips Brooks stated: 'Truth is always strong, no matter how weak it looks, and falsehood is always weak, no matter how strong it looks.'

References:

1. I have received a Christian pamphlet which argues along those very lines.

2. Francis Schaeffer, *How Should We Then Live?* Old Tappan, New Jersey: Fleming H. Revell Company, 1976, p.105.

3. A. C. Grayling, *What is Good?*, London: Phoenix, 2004, p.237.

4. Calvin, *Institutes*, IV.20.9.

5. Allan Bloom, *The Closing of the American Mind*, London: Penguin Books, 1987, pp.25-26.

6. Rosaria Champagne Butterfield, *The Secret Thoughts of an Unlikely Convert*, Pittsburgh: Crown & Covenant Publications, 2012, pp.87-88.

7. G. K. Chesterton, *Orthodoxy*, New York: Image Books, 1908, reprinted 1959, p.31, 32.

8. Francis Schaeffer, *The Great Evangelical Disaster*, Illinois: Crossway Books, 1948, p.48.

9. Noel Weeks, 'The Marxist Resurgence and its Three Stepchildren' in *Quadrant online*, 29 September 2017.

10. See Salvatore Babones, *The New Authoritarianism: Trump, Populism, and the Tyranny of Experts*, Medford: Polity Press, 2019, p.40.

11. Cited in Roger Scruton, *Fools, Frauds and Firebrands: Thinkers of the New Left*, London: Bloomsbury, 2015, p.9.

12. Fedor Dostoyevsky, *The Devils*, Victoria: Penguin, 1975, pp.421-422.

13. Simon Sebag Montefiore, *Young Stalin*, London: Phoenix, 2008.

14. See Eleanor Hancock, *Ernst Ruhm: Hitler's SA Chief of Staff*, New York: Palgrave Macmillan, 2008.

15. *Ibid.*, pp.14-15.

16. *Ibid.*, p.85.

17. *Ibid.*, p.89.

18   *Ibid.*, pp.115-116.

19   Charles Dickens, *Bleak House*, New York: New American Library, reprinted 1964, chapter XXXIX, p.555.

20   Rodney Croome, 'The threat-to-freedom narrative is just a bid for power and privilege', Opinion, *The Guardian*, 2 November 2017.

21   Thomas Watson, *The Ten Commandments*, Edinburgh: Banner of Truth, 1692, 1976, p.45.

22   George Orwell, *Nineteen Eighty-Four*, p.227.

23   Eric Metaxas, Bonhoeffer: Pastor. Martyr, Prophet, Spy, Nashville: Thomas Nelson, 2010, p.187.

24   Cited in Greg Lukianoff and Jonathan Haidt, *The Coddling of the American Mind,* Penguin, 2019, p.66.

25   Cited in Warren W. Wiersbe, *With the Word,* Nashville: Thomas Nelson, 1991, p.841.

Rev Dr Peter Barnes is Moderator-General of the Presbyterian Church of Australia and Pastor at Revesby Presbyterian Church

4

The Church is Under Attack

Judy Russell

As I see current world events accelerating, thereby heralding the return of our Lord Jesus Christ, rather than becoming dispirited or anxious I become excited. Jesus tells us that when we see these things occurring to look up as our redemption draws nigh (Luke 21:28).

Yes, the Church is under attack but, conversely, we see how the Church strengthens and grows when it is persecuted. Satan's wrath will not breach a Church built upon the unadulterated Word of God unless the attacks come from within. A Church built on the Rock will ultimately be a victorious Church.

Colin Stott of Global Recordings Network USA writes: "The Church of Jesus Christ, despite all of its appalling failures and sins, is the greatest force on earth for good and the only threat to Satan's Kingdom. It is the only group of people on the planet feared by the god of this age. No other religion poses any threat to him. None. Just the Church. Satan trembles when he hears God's people praising their Lord. Even the weakest saint on his or her knees surely strikes fear in the enemy camp.

"No surprise then that the Church is always under attack. This is especially true today as persecutions and unspeakable horrors are befalling many of our Christian brothers and sisters around the world. We see also the abominations of today's culture impacting our nations as a flood of evil threatens to overwhelm and marginalize the Church. Sadly, instead of influencing our culture for good, the Church finds itself being influenced by it.

"How are we to respond? Such times call for us to confess that we have not been the purified Bride that God intends us to be. Nor have we been the salt and light necessary to restrain evil in our society. More than ever do we need to humble ourselves, repent and pray and turn from our sinful ways (2 Chronicles 7:14)".

Jesus knew that Satan would attack His Bride and warned us very early on. Just as He pronounced a blessing upon Peter proclaiming his answer as recorded in Matthew 16:17-18 as divinely inspired, He will bless His Church today if she continues to faithfully seek after righteousness, preach the Gospel and proclaim His Word in full truth. *"And I say also unto thee, Thou art Peter, and upon this rock I will build my Church; and the gates of hell shall not prevail against it"*. **Satan has no power over an individual or a church that shelters under the blood of Jesus Christ and the truth and leading of the Holy Spirit.**

Why is the Church so weak in parts today? The early Church was Jewish. Jesus was and is Jewish - the Lion of the Tribe of Judah (Revelation 5:5). Catastrophically the Church of today has lost its 'Jewishness'. I often quote this little poem as I am thankful for its simple but profound truth. The first line is attributed to William Norman Ewer and the rest of the poem to Cecil Brown.

HOW ODD OF GOD TO CHOOSE THE JEWS

BUT ODDER STILL ARE THOSE WHO CHOOSE THE JEWISH GOD

BUT SPURN THE JEWS

Is the Church interpreting the times? Could that area of the Church that is buckling under Satan's attacks be a malnourished

Church, not feeding upon the whole Word of God from Genesis to Revelation? When we are malnourished, we are susceptible to attack by a creeping malaise, weakness leading to illness which, in turn, can lead to paralysis or even death. Jesus told the Pharisees and Sadducees that they did not know the times in which they lived. Do we? In Matthew 16, Jesus spoke these words *"But He replied, "When evening comes, you say, 'The weather will be fair, for the sky is red,' and in the morning, 'Today it will be stormy, for the sky is red and overcast.' You know how to interpret the appearance of the sky, but not the signs of the times. A wicked and adulterous generation demands a sign, but none will be given it except the sign of Jonah'.* Then He left them and went away.

One of the most exciting pointers to the times is the return of the Jewish nation to Israel, a factor so many in the Church continue to miss. Is this the time of the fig tree and all the trees sprouting leaves? (Luke 21:29-31).

How many in the Church neglect to pray for Israel and teach the signs of the times as outlined in the prophetic Scriptures? Many of these prophesies are spiritualised by some when in fact they are a manifesting observable fact, occurring before the eyes of those who wish to see. The Lord, as He promised, is bringing His people back to the land He covenanted to them. God does not break covenant.

Does the Church wish to step into her fullness? Through His suffering upon the Cross Jesus engrafted us into the Olive Tree (Romans 9-11). Do we wish to bless God and our older Jewish brethren by praying for His chosen people with whom God has kept covenant despite their unfaithfulness? Do we wish to bless His people and in turn be blessed? (Genesis 12:3).

In his book "The Mystery of the Olive Tree" Johannes Fichtenbauer writes: "It is not really possible to understand what the Church is, let alone talk about the 'Messianic Jewish phenomenon' without first being deeply confronted with the fact of Israel's election - Israel as the Apple of God's eye. The Church of the Gentiles will never reach the full measure of engagement with the plan of God on earth without understanding that it serves not just any God - but specifically the God of Israel. This has implications in all areas of our faith: in our theology and Christology, in our personal prayer life and our corporate worship, in our morals, in our evangelism, in the way we live out our family life in private and in the way that we are 'Church'".

God invites us to work with Him as He watches over His word to perform it (Jeremiah 1:12). He extends to us a glorious and exciting invitation. *"This is what the Sovereign Lord says: "See I will beckon to the Gentiles; I will lift up my banner to the peoples; they will bring your sons in their arms and carry your daughters on their shoulders"* (Isaiah 49:22-23a).

Our generation is the one privileged to see this prophesy occurring from the rebirth of the State of Israel in 1948. The rise in numbers of Messianic Jews in Israel is wonderful to behold. There are thousands of Jewish believers in the land of Israel today. Are we praying for the full number of Jews to come to faith in Yeshua/Jesus, their Messiah? Is Satan blinding the Church to this call? In our blindness are we delaying the return of Jesus to a world crying out for restoration?

Again, I quote from Colin Stott: "Such times call for us to identify the real enemy. It is not our leaders who disregard God's laws or those in the media or the politically correct brigade who mock us for our faith. Our fight is not against flesh and blood. No, our battle is with the powers of darkness that goad them to blaspheme the sacred and celebrate the obscene.

"As prayer warriors we must boldly rise up and take the fight to the heavenlies where the real battle is being waged. We have spiritual weapons to demolish strongholds of deception and every godless philosophy and false belief system that tries to exalt itself above the knowledge of God. (2 Corinthians 10:4-5). The Church, triumphant in Christ, must confront and destroy these if we are to see God's kingdom advance.

"And so, we keep our eyes fixed on Jesus. As the days get darker may our worship grow ever stronger. The more the enemy attacks the more praise God will receive! And let us show God's love to those who rage against the Church and who want to silence it. (How they must fear the Truth!) This is no time to retreat but to step up our intercession for the persecuted Church and for God to be glorified among the nations. His honour matters!"

Should we worry about cancel culture and woke-ism? Let the word of God answer our question. *"I have told you these things, so that in me you may have peace. In this world you will have trouble. But take heart! I have overcome the world"* (John 16:33).

I finish this chapter by again referring to the Lord and His work in Israel and the nations. The Gospel went out to the ends of the earth from Jerusalem, and it is returning to the land in a wonderful and exciting way. There are marvellous ministries at work in Israel. Let the Church *"Pray for the peace of Jerusalem, they shall prosper that love thee"* (Psalm 122:6).

***

Judy Russell is the Coordinator of *Christian Worldview* which hosts speakers from Australia and internationally on Judeo-Christian issues.

5

Woke-ism its Origins and its Effect on the Christian Church

Ettienne McClintock

At the turn of this century no one would have predicted that Australian Christians would be attacked for writing about the values most Australians believed only two decades ago.

Within our societies we find a new type of 'justice', a wokeness that is promoted in the media, in educational institutions and governmental circles. This new social justice is diametrically opposed to the principles of God's kingdom as spoken by God Himself at Mt Sinai and taught by Jesus. God's moral code is considered offensive and even oppressive by the woke who will do anything they can to silence any person who dares to bear witness to the Truth. Within this movement we see the early signs of persecution in Australia. How is it possible that these moral principles based on Divine love can be shunned and despised by those it intends to bless? This purest form of love was demonstrated in Christ's death for the weak, the ungodly, for sinners and even God's enemies (Romans 5:6, 8, 10).

So much has changed in the last 100 years when we consider that in the first Australian census of 1901, 96% of the Australians identified as Christian. As the Australian population grew and prospered, the number of Christians as a percentage gradually declined. Twelve censuses' later when the population had grown threefold to 11.6 million the census of 1966 showed that a just over 88% of people in Australia were Christian. Fast forward to the 2011 census and the percentage had declined to 60%. But what happened during the next five-year period to 2016 is staggering. The 2016 census showed a decline of 8% in five short years.

While we may be surprised by the rapid decline of Christianity in our society, we know One that has not been surprised by any of this. As Christians we serve a God that has always known the future and has seen the end of each event from its very beginning (Isaiah 46:10). God inspired the Apostle Paul to predict the spiritual and societal conditions for our times. Reading 2nd Timothy 3:1-4 we see a clear description of our society today. *"But know this, that in the last days of earth's history dangerous times will come because mankind will love only themselves and their pursuits after wealth. They will be proud and boastful; they will blaspheme God and disobey their parents. They will be ungrateful for the blessings they have. They will oppose holiness and hate members of their own society. They will slander anyone who disagrees with them and will refuse to forgive anyone. They will become brutes without any self-restraint. They will despise good things and betray anyone they disagree with. They will be highly arrogant and confident of their own opinions. They will pursue their own pleasures because their love is only inwardly focussed, and they will reject their love for God."* This is an accurate description of our society today.

God's Word has further insights in identifying the dark forces and influencers that would shape societal conditions and lead an attack on Christianity and Christian values. The Book of Revelation which shows the history and future of the New Testament church gives us some further remarkable insights.

When we look at Revelation 11, we see there a Beast that is released out of the bottomless pit. It is a Beast designed for spiritual warfare and he makes war with God's two Witnesses and ends up overpowering and killing them. It shows contempt even for their dead bodies and does not even provide a burial for them. We are told that they die in one of the two "the great cities" mentioned in Revelation. The city where their death occurs is the great opposing movement against God's kingdom called Babylon (Rev 14:8). The other city is the great city of God called "the holy Jerusalem" (Rev 21:10).

The identifying characteristics of Babylon are that it aligns with Sodom and Egypt in a spiritual sense (Rev 11:8). In Bible history Sodom was known for sexual immorality which included same sex attraction (Jude 1:7). Egypt is known as the power that enslaved God's people for a 400-year period. The head of this nation was Pharaoh who declared himself an atheist and insubordinate to God's authority. He refused to acknowledge the existence and sovereignty of God when he said: *"Who is the Lord that I should obey His voice to let Israel go? I do not know the Lord, nor will I let Israel go"* **Genesis 5:2.**

What do these two identifying marks of Babylon tell us about the societal conditions promoted to kill God's two witnesses? Sodom aligning with modern day sexual immorality as promoted by the LGBTIQA+ movement, and Egypt aligns with atheism. We see these opposing forces as the main drivers in waring against God's two Witnesses.

Revelation 11 tells us that the Two Witnesses are the two Olive Trees and the Two Lampstands who stand before the God of the earth. The Old Testament prophet Zechariah identified the two Olive Trees as *"the Word of the Lord"* Zechariah 4:3-6. But in the OT, there was only one Lampstand with seven branches. In the NT era we see two Lampstands signifying the addition of another witness. This can easily be identified as the additional witness of the New Testament.

What then does it mean to kill God's two Witnesses? Revelation 11 tells us that the beast from the bottomless pit makes *"war against"* God's two Witnesses and *"overcomes them"*. The same language is used to describe the persecution of God's people in Daniel 7:21 and Revelation 13:7 where it describes another beast, this time coming from the sea, who would also *"make war with God's saints and overcome them"*. The beastly power from the bottomless pit persecuted God's people with the aim of shutting down their witness for Christ and His Word (see John 15:20). This power appears to succeed in its objective of shutting down their testimony but only for a short period. Here we see that the witness of God's people would be extinguished for a time in the public arena through cancel culture and de-platforming.

But what does a Beast represent in Bible prophecy and who is behind this Beast?

The prophet Daniel tells us that a Beast in prophecy refers to a King (Dan 7:17) or a Kingdom (v23) which means we are dealing with a political power. Who or what is behind this political power that ascends out of the bottomless pit? Who releases it from the bottomless pit?

Two chapters earlier in Revelation we are introduced to an entity that received the keys to the bottomless pit. This entity was known as a fallen star from heaven (Rev 9:1). It was this same entity that opened the bottomless pit (v2). To know what a star represents we must read the first chapter of Revelation that tells us that a star represents an Angel (Rev 1:20). But this angel that has the keys to the bottomless pit is not just any angel. This angel is represented as a star fallen from heaven and a fallen star must refer to a fallen angel. In chapter 12 we read that the dragon and his angels fought with Michael and His angels in heaven but the dragon who is the devil and Satan was cast out from heaven to the earth. Jesus said in Luke 10:18 that he *"saw satan fall like lightening from heaven".*

The entity identified in the Bible that empowers this beast from the bottomless pit that makes war on God's Word and His people is none other than Satan, the adversary of Christ. Satan has been very successful in shutting down the witness for Christ and His Truth in western countries. The latest polls show that less than 50% of Australians identify as Christian (McCrindle - Australia's Changing Spiritual Climate, 2021). At the same time the data shows that about one third of Australians identify as atheists.

When the old historicist lens of interpretation is applied to Revelation, a method that the Reformers also employed, we see that many scholars identify the events of Revelations 11 as the beginnings of modern Atheism which started in France. During the French revolution, in 1793, *"the world for the first time heard an assembly of men, born and educated in civilization, and assuming the right to govern one of the finest of the European nations, uplift their united voice to deny the most solemn truth which man's soul receives, and renounce unanimously the belief and worship of a Deity"*, Sir Walter Scott, *Life of Napoleon,* vol.1, Ch 17. This is an echo of the same mindset of the Pharoah of Egypt. We also read in Blackwood's Magazine of November 1870 that *"France stands apart in the world's history as the single state which, by the decree of her Legislative Assembly, pronounced that there was no God, and of which the entire population of the capital, and a vast majority elsewhere, women as well as men, danced and sang with joy in accepting the announcement".*

The teachings of Marxism developed during this era of Atheism. It was only 55 years later that Karl Max and Friedrich Engels published the Communist Manifesto. The militant application of Marxism was adopted and applied as Communism in 1917 by Lenin in the Soviet Union. While Communism appeared to collapse in 1989 with the fall of the USSR, five communist regimes remain with China being the most prominent of them all.

The false promises of freedom embodied in Marxist teachings has been adequately demonstrated by Communism. However, the philosophical aspects of Marxism have become very popular and is now taught in our primary schools, high schools, and universities. It is almost exclusively promoted through the mainstream media and all forms of secular entertainment.

The Beast from the bottomless pit represents modern day atheism and makes war on God's Word. This power is clearly demonstrated to be satanic in origin. It is no wonder that the atheism promoted by Marxism also has the same hellish power behind it as seen in the writings of its author.

Marxism has had a modern-day makeover and morphed into cultural Marxism. The economic class struggle espoused by Marx when he wrote about the oppression of the Proletariat (the workers) by the Bourgeoisie (the capitalists) has been modified and adapted to take on new identity wars. It's no longer just about economics. Oppression has been redefined through the identification of new victim groups not considered to be such in bygone years. Communism showed that the promised utopia where everyone was guaranteed equal outcomes regardless of their abilities, commitment or education was false. While militant Marxism failed to provide the freedom, it promised to the masses its principles live on through social justice.

The Bible speaks for the oppressed and advocates justice for all based on the principles of righteousness or right-doing. Psalms 119:172 says: *"My tongue shall speak of Your Word for all your commandments are righteousness"*. Those who truly stand for Justice and Righteousness will continue to speak God's Word and the constitution of Heaven, His Commandments.

There are two Hebrew words in the Bible which are commonly used to express the concept of justice. These are mishpat, used

421 times and tsedaqah used 157 times. Both these words are not only translated as 'justice' but often translated as 'righteousness'. The Bible does not separate justice from righteousness. If God's Word including all His commandments encapsulate true justice and righteousness, why do we find so much opposition to Biblical righteousness from the woke community and their Social Justice Warriors? When you oppose righteousness, you replace it with unrighteousness and according to 1 John 5:17 *"all unrighteousness is sin"*. Does the social justice movement promote sin while it claims a form of godliness or right doing? Does it promote a so-called justice that is contrary to God's law of love? 1 John 3:4 defines *"sin as lawlessness"*. The KJV Bible translates this same passage as *"sin is the transgression of the law"*. Have we not seen a lawless element to the BLM protests/riots and their quest to defund the police? The BLM leaders have publicly said that they are trained Marxists.

As Christians we oppose all forms of racism because it's condemned by the Word of God. We see an example of this in the family quarrel that Aaron and Miriam had with their younger brother Moses over his wife. God reproved them both for their racist attitude towards Moses' wife because she was a dark skinned Ethiopian (Numbers 12:1-2). But is this the racism that social justice also opposes? If so, why is it that Critical Race Theory (CRT) identifies all white cis gender males as racist and sexist and victimisers simply because of their gender identity and the colour of their skin.

This woke attitude was demonstrated in March 2021 at Brauer College in Victoria when all male students were asked to stand up in an assembly and apologise for their gender in the wake of the justice for women movement. A similar incident happened a month later at Melbourne's Parkdale Secondary College when a Kingston Council social worker spoke about privilege, pronouns, and intersectionality. During the presentation, boys who were straight, white, and Christian were asked to stand up in front of their peers. They were then told they were responsible for being "oppressors" because of their white privilege.

CRT sees oppression through a prism of power where oppression flows from the top down, but it never flows from the bottom up. While apparently seeking equality and equal outcomes for all they promote another inequality. They identify white cis gender males as oppressors irrespective of their behaviour or the content of their character. CRT teaches that white cis gender males oppress everyone below them on this social totem pole. This includes white cis gender females who in turn oppress black cis gender males who in turn oppress black cis gender females. They all in turn are oppressors of gays and lesbians, who in turn are oppressors of transgender and non-binary individuals and so it goes on. As mentioned before, within this model of oppression, discrimination can only flow from the top down it cannot flow upward from the oppressed. You can be targeted and called a racist simply for being white even though you may treat all races as equal. It is important to note that the current BLM movement is not based on the same principles espoused by Dr Martin Luther King when he said in his famous speech on 28 August 1963, at the Lincoln Memorial in Washington D.C: *"I have a dream that my four little children will one day live in a nation where they will not be judged by the colour of their skin but by the content of their character."*

This same wokeness born out of cultural Marxism has identified homosexual couples as victims of oppression. They took it a step further and claimed dissatisfaction with the terms of a civil union already afforded to gay couples. They desired the same marital status afforded to heterosexual married couples. This meant that marriage which was 1st instigated and defined by God in Eden as a union between one man and one woman had to be redefined to include same sex partnerships. Many warned that the redefining of marriage would end up removing the freedom of Christians to freely witness for the principles of righteousness as defined in God's Word. Freedom of speech which is a fundamental right of any free society would be lost. If their same sex union did not meet the definition of marriage, why not just call it something else? Unfortunately, the warnings went unheeded. Attempting to bring about equal outcomes contrary to Biblical right doing was and always has been a social recipe for disaster. The Bible tells us in Proverbs 14:34 that *"righteousness exalts a nation, but sin is a reproach to any people"*.

In 2017 Australia as a nation rejected the millennia old definition of marriage as the union of one male and one female in holy matrimony. They set God's commandments aside and *"exchanged the truth of God for the lie and worshiped the (opinions of the) creature rather than the Creator"*, **Romans 1:25**. The woke SJW's ignored a very important component. Marriage as defined by God in His Word is designed to make a married couple one flesh. The full expression of "one flesh" is ultimately seen in producing one flesh, or a baby, from the two. According to Malachi 2:15, God made male and female one, because he was seeking godly offspring from the marriage union.

This woke move against traditional marriage and the family unit was an act of defiance against God. God was the One Who first defined marriage at creation, but this fact was ignored and was put to a public vote. Cultural Marxism had successfully infiltrated a big part of Australian society and when the postal vote was finally counted 61.7% of Australians voted in support of same sex marriage in the 2017. Since this time there has been a growing disregard for free speech in Australia. People who have shared the universal truths of God's Word based on their own convictions have found themselves in opposition to the new woke morality. The list of people who have been de-platformed, cancelled and have even lost their jobs is growing.

In 2019 Dr Jereth Kok was suspended from medical practice over sharing his Christian beliefs online about abortion and LGBT issues.

International Rugby player Israel Folau had his employment terminated by posting that all sinners who do not repent would end up in hell. His 'sin' in pointing out a list of sins, was to include homosexuality in that list.

Margaret Court the greatest tennis player of all time continues to be de-platformed and derided for her Biblical views on marriage. She is especially targeted every year during the Australian Tennis Open when they won't even allow her to speak at the tournament. Her 'sin' was writing an open letter to Qantas to voice her disappointment at the airline's promotion of same sex marriage in the lead up to the 2017 postal vote.

The negative publicity and pressures put on these Christians through cancel culture has caused many to reconsider their own public witness for Truth. Many are now practicing self-censorship in the public arena.

Persecution often starts with its milder forms on the persecution scale. The intent of the persecutor is always to shut down a Christians witness for Christ and His Truth. It often starts with ridicule, harassment, discrimination, and public attacks. If these forms of persecution do not silence God's witnesses, they resort to more severe forms. Laws are passed to fine Christians and boycott them economically. If these oppressive methods don't work further laws are passed with penalties of imprisonment. In many countries torture and death are used as tools of oppression to silence Christians from sharing Christ openly or even privately. When people are motivated by the principle of God's love even the use of harsher forms of persecution like torture is unable to break their spirit. Some will ultimately end up witnessing for the Truth through their spilled blood in martyrdom. But these Christians are encouraged by Jesus words that those *"who lose their life for Christ's sake and the Gospel's will find it"*, Mark 8:35.

The question is, what will you and I do when faced with these choices? Will we continue to love Christ with that perfect love that casts out fear (1 John 4:18)? Or will we surrender our witness for the sake of our temporal wellbeing?

***

Ettienne McClintock is the Director of Communications at Voice of the Martyrs Australia

6

Understanding the Cause of the Attack on Christianity

Bernard Gaynor

You have probably never thought about this, and you may instinctively disagree. But the modern concept of 'freedom of religion' is the primary reason Christians in Australia are losing their religious freedom today.

As the idea is practically understood in the modern world, 'freedom of religion' really means 'freedom of religions'. More precisely, it means freedom of false religions. And this is dangerous, objectively evil and at odds with the most basic law of logic: the law of non-contradiction.

So, let's start at the start and understand what we truly should be striving for. And that is most certainly not freedom of false religions. Instead, every society including ours should be striving for freedom of the true religion.

This essay does not provide the time, place, or space to address which religion is the true religion but suffice to say here that I am Catholic, and I write with a Catholic perspective. But this fact is not central to the main theme of this essay.

I hope that you will take from this essay these three points:

Firstly, there can only one true religion. Secondly, the civil authorities have an obligation to recognise the true religion and to provide for its freedom. Thirdly, the civil authorities have the moral authority and a duty to the common good to suppress false religions to the extent that they undermine societal cohesion and safety.

A society that does these three things will provide true freedom of religion. A society that does not will either place false religions on the same level as the true religion (which is objectively evil and will necessarily impede true religious freedom) or it will mandate false religions (which is worse and will destroy true religious freedom entirely). It should also go without saying that the former tends to the latter. That's because any society that gives error the same rights as truth is already at war with it and will eventually seek to destroy truth altogether.

As a matter of logic, we can know with certainty that there can only be one true religion. The law of non-contradiction is that contradictory statements cannot simultaneously be true. This is self-evident. A thing cannot be some particular thing and at the same time is not that particular thing. Or, in other words, I cannot be a man and not be a man at the same time.

The same goes for religion. A religion provides a system of worship of a god or gods based on doctrine and theology which expresses 'true' statements about the divinity.

Now, the theology of each religion cannot be true and not be true at the same time. Yet each religion directly contradicts every other religion. For example, Christianity teaches that God has three persons. Islam rejects the Trinity. Both doctrines cannot be simultaneously true and false.

Even within denominations, there is contradiction. Catholics believe in the real presence at the Holy Sacrifice of the Mass. Most other Christians do not. They cannot both be true. There are other differences. The Catholic Church teaches, for example, that contraception is gravely evil. Again, most other Christian denominations do not. Again, they cannot both be correct.

Man is a rational being. He has been created with an ability to reason. He can know with certainty that where religions contradict each other, only one can be true.

These contradictions are not minor differences either. They go to the very question of who God is or to the question of good and evil. These differences are fundamentally important and cannot simply be wished away. It is no answer to the cold light of logic to claim that each religion expresses some fundamental truth in its own way. What truth would that be? That question cannot be answered without addressing these differences head on.

There are other problems with this thinking too. With his reason, man has an additional foundation on which to be certain that there can only be one true religion. This comes from his ability to gain some natural understanding of God's existence and nature. Man can reason the existence of God and there are various proofs of this perhaps the best of which were articulated by St Thomas Aquinas in the 13th Century. However, pre-Christian philosophers such as Aristotle also reasoned the existence of a perfect God who was all powerful, all knowing and unchanging, which also means that God is Truth.

God cannot deceive or be deceived. Thus, the idea that God has created various religions of a contradictory nature is repugnant to the very essence of what God is. If God exists (and we can reason that He does) then there must be a true religion which expresses the theology of God based on natural reason and any revelation beyond that which He may have given to us.

The civil authorities and the state have an obligation to recognise this true religion, which is another way of saying that the civil authorities and the state have an obligation to recognise God.

We can reason this in two ways: by understanding the nature of man and understanding the nature of the state. Each person has been given intelligence and his senses to understand what he can about God and to give Him worship. But man is also a social being. He lives in a community. Therefore, he must by his very nature worship God individually and as part of society. It is absurd to say that man, as an individual, is required to practise the true religion but within the community of men can ignore God completely. Equally, it is incongruous to claim that God demands that we do good and avoid evil as individuals but cares little for our moral behaviour as social beings.

The true religion encompasses our social activity just as much as it does our private lives. It does so because morality applies to our collective and public actions just as much as it does to our private works. Those who disagree may just as well argue that morality does not happen in public, or that good or evil are confined to the home. And that is a patently laughable proposition.

The nature of the state also demands a collective recognition of God. For a start, the state is a creation of God, just as much as we are created individually. Sure, each person may have some input into the development of his society, but it still exists, just as each of us do, entirely because of God's creative work. From this very fact alone, the state is duty bound to recognise its creator. It is an injustice to refuse to do so on the erroneous basis that the state cannot identify the true religion, just as it is irrational to claim that an individual in a position of authority must recognise God privately but is free to reject Him publicly.

The state and the civil authorities are also nothing more than the natural ordering of the community of men. This authority derives from God. Again, the state is duty bound to provide due recognition of this fact and, again, it is an injustice not to do so. Indeed, the state must go further than this: its very purpose is to provide order for the common good of men which means it has an obligation to enact laws which give liberty to the true religion, both for the private worship of each man and so that all can worship as a social being. Conversely, it is an injustice for the state to enact laws which provide official recognition of false religion or to direct resources in support of those religions.

From this, it also follows that the state has a role to play in suppressing false religion. This is not to say that the state should be a theocracy or that it has authority to coerce religious belief, even in the true religion. Such an exercise of power would be contrary to the natural order of creation and free will that God gave each man. However, it must be acknowledged that the state has legitimate moral authority to act to protect the common good and it is duty bound to do so where false religion undermines the common good.

The state can tolerate false religion where it does not undermine social cohesion. A religion which was based on erroneous theology, but which encouraged the practice of natural virtue and morality does not pose a threat to society or endanger lives. It can be tolerated. However, this cannot be said about all religions. Some encourage their spread using violence. Others promote gravely evil behaviours which endanger life and limb. Still others claim all authority to themselves, including civil authority.

The state is duty bound to suppress these false religions and it must do so to the extent that these false religions pose a threat to the state and the common good.

Given all the above, it is now much easier to understand where we are in Australia today, why Christians are constantly under attack and why efforts to protect their freedom have not only failed but inevitably worsen the situation.

Australia has had a distinctively Christian heritage which has shaped its laws, culture, and institutions. However, denominational differences have multiplied, leading to a loss of coherence around even the basic tenets of Christian belief. A prudent determination to avoid sectarianism set the scene for modern anti-discrimination laws which dictate that all beliefs are to be treated as equally valid. This has broadened from a general understanding that religion in Australia had a Christian flavour to government policy at the state and Commonwealth level since at least the 1970s which pretended that other religions were on the same level as Christianity. We now have Satanists demanding the right carry out their sacrilegious and evil activities in public buildings.

Many people believed that this was approach would provide religious freedom. But unfortunately, it has done nothing of the sort. It was an illusory freedom based on the fraudulent notion that there is no knowable truth, no true religion, and no necessity for the state to recognise it or even God Himself. It was a revolt of our society against God in favour of error and evil.

A temporary peace has lasted while the cultural legacy of Christianity held this revolution in check. But the phoney war has now ended. Those who promote error and evil are no longer satisfied with simply being placed on the same level as truth and goodness. So, they are now attempting, by force of law, to suppress it entirely. They demand it because the darkness cannot tolerate any light.

Christians in Australia cannot combat this attack by clinging to the very system that has unleashed this assault on truth. Christians will not be granted religious freedom through further additions to anti-discrimination law because these laws are designed specifically not to recognise God or truth.

If Christians want true religious freedom, they need to quit the pretence that any form of Christianity is valid. Then they need to understand that their fight is not to be treated like other non-Christian religions but to have the true Christian faith recognised officially by the state. The poison ideas that have permeated our understanding of 'religious freedom' need to be discarded.

If Christianity is the true religion, and I believe it is as taught by the Catholic Church, then we need to work for it and it alone to be recognised by the state. Our goal should be to have Christ recognised as our nation's king, as he truly is. And if we reach that conclusion, then the confusion we entangle ourselves in within this debate will evaporate. We do not need careful laws that balance competing rights, beliefs, and moral systems. We only need laws that give liberty to truth. Everything else can be tolerated or not, depending on its impact on the common good of our society.

I do not know how to achieve this politically. Indeed, I am pessimistic about any prospect of success in the short term. I fear our society has fallen so far that it will only find truth on its knees, just as we all fall on our knees in times of great need. But God is all powerful and we should not forget that.

***

Bernard Gaynor is a social commentator and has been subjected to both woke and cancel culture by the LGBTIQA+ activists and the Australian Army.

7

The Devil is Always in the Detail

Rev. Hon. Fred Nile MLC

We have seen time and time again 'Cancel Culture' targeting the Church, Christian philosophy, and Christian views. Getting 'Cancelled' is the process by which someone is thrust out of social or professional circles – it mainly occurs online or on social media and has been coined by millennials caught up in the frenzy of 'Cancel Culture'. 'Cancel Culture' is the weapon of choice used by the 'Cultural Revolution' whose primary agenda is to normalise LGBTQIA+ ideals. The only way it can do that is by obliterating its opposition, the Church. The questions we should be asking are, how did the 'Cultural Revolution' attain such momentum and power? And what can we do about it?

There seems to be an almost inverse relationship between the rise of Anti-discrimination legislation and the fall of our rights to free thought, free speech and freedom of religion. You can see the direct correlation between the mounting anti-discrimination reforms and the advance of the 'Cultural Revolution'. It almost seemed that the 'Cultural Revolution' was arming itself with the necessary laws it needed to take down conservative Christian views, values, and beliefs.

When Prime Minister Gough Whitlam introduced the *Racial Discrimination Act 1975* we all applauded. Section 9 of the act states "It is unlawful for a person to do any act involving a distinction, exclusion, restriction or preference based on race, colour, descent or national or ethnic origin which has the purpose or effect of nullifying or impairing the recognition, enjoyment or exercise, on an equal footing, of any human right or fundamental freedom in the political, economic, social, cultural or any other field of public life."[1]

As Christians we are all made in the image of God, so we agree that all people are equal. At last, we thought Christian philosophy is being entrenched in secular law, so we thought. But then comes section 18C of the Racial Discrimination Act which makes it illegal to carry out an act if: "(a) the act is reasonably likely, in all the circumstances, to offend, insult, humiliate or intimidate another person or a group of people; and (b) the act is done because of the race, colour or national or ethnic origin of the other person or of some or all of the people in the group".[2]

At first glance we say "it's not right to hurt someone's feelings" but the definition outlined in 18C is so broad and subjective, it goes beyond saving someone's feelings. It gives anyone the unilateral right to place a gagging order on anyone saying or thinking differently to them. We neglected to read the fine print and the Devil is always in the detail.

Everyone has heard the phrase "Sticks and stones may break my bones, but words will never hurt me" but what people don't know is the true meaning behind this adage. One of its earliest sightings was in The Christian Recorder of March 1862, a publication of the African Methodist Episcopal Church, where it is presented in this form: "Sticks and stones may break my bones, but words will never break me. But names will never harm me".[3] The saying was aimed at defeating the victim mentality and ending the endless cycle of revenge. It grew out of the teaching of the gospel where Jesus Christ from the Sermon on the Mount gave an alternative solution to "an eye for an eye". Christ said "if anyone slaps you on the right cheek, turn to him the other also. And if anyone would sue you and take your tunic, let him have your cloak as well" (Matthew 5:38-42, NIV Version). Even the bible warns us about the about the endless cycles of litigation spawned by revenge and anger. Engaging in endless battle whether physical or verbal will never end discrimination only forgiveness can do that.

If 18C only enables endless litigation, why have it? That's because the 'Cultural Revolution' lobbied hard for it. It equips minority groups with the ability to battle what most of the population believes in, with the aim of annihilating the opposition's beliefs.

If you look at Australia's demographics in 1975 when the anti-discrimination law first came into being, Christianity dominated the landscape, most people believed that marriage was only between a man and a woman, and the concept of euthanasia was considered to be murder. Fast forward to today and being Christian is considered backward, marriage can take place between two people who identify in a myriad of sexualities and euthanasia is considered an act of compassion.

Next came *The Sex Discrimination Act 1984*. This act aimed to eliminate all forms of discrimination against women.[4]

How beneficial has this law really been for women? Well as soon as it was a given that most women could work full time, the first thing banks did was change how they assessed housing loans. No longer did they calculate a loan assessment on the husband's income alone, now a wife's income became a mandatory inclusion. This meant to get a housing loan you needed to show a higher income than before, to get a loan large enough to purchase a house. Now whether a woman wanted to or not, she had to work full time to pay the mortgage. I see that as a loss of choice not a gain.

As double income assessed housing loans became more

common, this in-turn increased housing prices. This poured even more pressure on women to stay in work even when they had children. They no longer had the luxury of opting out of work for years on end to raise their children. Women were forced to work a full-time job, place the children in day care and then come home and cook and clean. I don't see how this can be seen as giving women equal opportunities to men. When you combine the paid work and home duties they must fulfil, they end up working longer hours than men and the opportunity cost of forgoing raising their children is a great cost not only to them but to society as a whole.

The other loser in this equation are children. Day care centres can't replicate the one-on-one care and nurturing only a mother can offer her child in its formative years. American academic Jay Belsky's 1986 study *Infant Day care: A Cause for Concern?* warned that babies who were looked after in day care were showing signs of increased levels of aggression and disobedience in later life.[5]

Sex discrimination legislation has indirectly contributed to the corruption and decay of morality in our children and the destruction of the family unit. Christian philosophy is disseminated to children from parents. As the bonds of the family falter, children are no longer taught the true and righteous path and are seduced by left leaning ideologies that dominate secular society.

For the Sex Discrimination Act to truly be fairer and give women more opportunities it should have offered maternity leave till children were old enough to attend kindergarten. This would have given women a true choice. Government reasoning for objecting to lengthy maternity leave was cost and yet they subsidised childcare providers to the tune of hundreds of millions of dollars. This money could have gone directly to mothers, affording them the ability to stay at home and raise their own children.

In 2013 The Sex Discrimination Act was amended to include *(Sexual Orientation, Gender Identity, and Intersex Status)* with this act the 'rainbow revolution' had arrived. The critical change I need to highlight in this piece of legislation, is the omission of "marital status" and its substitution with "sexual orientation, gender identity, intersex status, marital or relationship status."[6] When this legislation came into effect, I could not help but feel that the next target for the gender political movement would be conventional marriage. Now that you were prohibited from questioning same sex marriage there was nothing stopping its legalisation by the Federal Parliament in December 2017.

The LGBTQIA+ movement aided and abetted by mainstream media had reached critical mass. It was now out leashing its gender fluid ideology in governments, workplaces, schools, television and online. You either conformed to this way of thinking or faced the wrath of 'Cancel Culture'.

Now to get 'Cancelled' doesn't take much. Paraphrasing the Bible got Israel Folau booted out of Rugby Australia. Corey Feldman (former child actor) was the first who told everyone about the sexual abuse going on with child actors in Hollywood, and no one listened. Barbara Walters yelled at him for exposing it.[7] 'Cancelling' someone is a way of not allowing another person's point of view to be heard. And its usually large globalist organisations who want to quash your say, even if it's the truth.

In just a short time the LGBTQIA+ had achieved what it wanted, to be considered normal. In 2004 the ABC received enormous backlash for showing two mums on the iconic children's program Play School[8] but by 2021 there was barely a raised eyebrow when the ABC featured a drag queen interviewing kids about their sexuality. In fact, the ABC deleted its link to a LGBTQIA+ drag queen's Facebook page. But the "Little Kids, Big Talk – Gender" video, featuring a drag queen remains up on the ABC Kids Community Facebook page.

Evolutionary Scientists have stated that gender can't be fluid, it can't be non-binary but that did not stop the spread of these concepts in government programs such as Safe Schools[9] which Tony Abbott called a 'social engineering programme dressed up as anti-bullying'. The program was scrapped due to its negative reception but it was later replaced by the more ardent *The Good Society*.[10] This 'educational resource' has been made available to every Australian educator and student. Radical gender theory is rife throughout The Good Society, I quote: "*A person's gender is their sense of themselves in relation to their biological sex. A person's gender identity can be the same as their sex assigned at birth, or it can differ*".

I am a proud Father, Grandfather and Great Grandfather and I can assure you that a person's gender identity is very clearly defined from the moment their mother delivers them into this world. Our children should not be subject to the perverse ideological desires of warped adults. Children deserve our love, support, and prayers and very often that involves guidance from their mother and father down the right path or away from the wrong path. The Good Society encourages boys to experiment with gender fluidity by wearing women's shoes, this is the wrong path for our sons.

Anti-discrimination laws have been used by the 'Cultural Revolution' to censor Christian views out of print, radio, and television and now it's taking aim at our presence online.

Wikipedia touts itself as a free, multilingual online encyclopaedia written and maintained by a community of volunteer contributors.

It tends to leave out the fact that free thought, free speech, and a free platform is not on offer to contributors who have conservative viewpoints, instead their content is deleted, and blocks are placed on their IP addresses.

Wikipedia doesn't stop there, it;

- Deletes Christian sources it deems as "unreliable" or "promotional" or "spam" etc.
- Adds unflattering content to subtlety denigrate entries for those of the 'Right'
- Has thousands of pages on Left-wing trivia.
- Has a massive number of LGBTQIA+ pages - some with pornographic images.
- Interestingly, almost anything negative said about Islam, is banned.
- It replicates *Facebook* in what it deems as 'conspiracies'.

All this is done under Wikipedia's Guidelines.

Here are a couple of specific examples where Wikipedia has waved its censorship wand; Apologist and ethicist Bill Muehlenberg and Managing Director of the Australian Christian Lobby Martyn Iles have had their Wikipedia pages deleted as 'Not Notable'. Bill Muehlenberg was deleted on 15 December 2011 and Martyn Iles Wikipedia entry was deleted after May 2020 but is available via Web Archive.

Wikipedia has a Wikipedia-jury to 'adjudicate'. However, the Wikipedia-jury seems a bit to the Left of the Facebook Fact Checkers. 'Tis pointless appealing.

The co-founder of Wikipedia Larry Sanger, has said this about Wikipedia: "In short, and with few exceptions, only globalist, progressive mainstream sources—and sources friendly to globalist progressivism—are permitted."[11]

Sanger suggested that Wikipedia's editors have "systematically purged conservative mainstream media sources" because its editors "do not want what they dismiss as 'misinformation,' 'conspiracy theories,' etc. to get any hearing. In saying so, they (and similarly biased institutions) are plainly claiming exclusive control over what is thinkable. They want to set the boundaries of the debate, and they want to tell you how to think about it."[12]

Wokepedia! – Let's start by defining the word 'woke', the urban dictionary defines it as "illusory or false consciousness. The act of being overly pretentious about how much you care about a social issue."[13] The supposed idea of Wokepedia is that ordinary people, can make lasting changes to Wikipedia that will lead to more equitable and less biased coverage of topics of minority interest, and promote a raised level of consciousness among Wikipedia readers. The concept that anyone can be part of Wokepedia is the irony as we already know that conservative views are being filtered out.

Wikipedia has this image of championing free information but researcher Michael Olenick at INSEAD business school who is investigating the Foundation stated the following "People take it for granted that it is a sweet little charity that does nothing wrong and is totally harmless but none of that is true,"[14] ... "Wikipedia's operations, according to data collected require $10 million. And it could be done without them since any academic centre could give you the computing resources you need. The current fundraising campaign raised $142 million."[15]

If you are ever in the situation where you have noticed pages deleted from any particular website, you can always retrieve them through *Internet Archive – Wayback Machine*.[16] Just enter the website you are investigating and hit browse history, then select a date in the past when you last think you saw this information and presto you will be transported back in internet time history.

The bias against Christian content is not limited to Wikipedia. Google has a distinctive left leaning bias. An alternative search engine is *DuckDuckGo*. With *DuckDuckGo* you can search to find a plethora of Wikipedia Christian bias examples. You might test other conservative issues such as 'abortion' on *Google* vs *DuckDuckGo*.

Social media is also actively censoring Christian posts. Facebook blocks 'Christian Speech'. "A group of broadcasters wants US Congress to ask billionaire Zuckerberg about allegations Facebook routinely blocks images and content with a conservative message."

"What we're raising awareness of is that really across the board – Facebook, Twitter, Instagram, Google, GoFundMe, Apple, App Store – you've got really the censorship of Christian content and conservative content across the board," Dr Jerry Johnson, president and CEO of the National Religious, told CBN News."[17]

How do we change all this? With good legislation that allows Australian laws to fully realise their Judeo-Christian foundation. Most people reference Ancient Greece as the birthplace of democracy, but the government of that era was very different to that of today. In Ancient Greece only free men had a voice and the ability to vote. Women, children, and slaves were treated as chattel. It was only when the teachings of Christ arrived in Greece that true democracy was born. It was Christ who taught us to place value on women, children, the sick, the old and to free the slaves.

I am also reminded of William Wilberforce a member of the British Parliament and a devout Christian. God called him to this position to bring about the Slavery Abolition Act 1833. The Christian Democratic Party (CDP) followed in William Wilberforce's footsteps and managed the passage of the NSW

Modern Slavery Act 2018. The Australian Parliament inspired by what the CDP had achieved followed suit and brought out federal legislation on modern slavery.

I continue to put forward legislation that is inspired by Christian philosophy. Here is a list of legislation that is either in draft or we are currently working on: Public Health Amendment (Vaccine Compensation) Bill 2021, Children and Young Persons (Prohibition of Experimental Gender Reassignment Treatment) Amendment Bill 2021, Sex Selection Abortion Prohibition Bill, and the Fairness in Women's Sports Bill.

Of course, we can table new legislation, but bills can be defeated when it comes to the vote in Parliament. We need people to get behind Christian minded politicians and vote them in, so we not only have a one Christian voice in Parliament but a whole chorus. We need numbers if we want our battle for change to succeed. I use the term battle because we are in a state of war. We are battling between the forces of good and evil. God wants us to hear him, because only through the gospel can people be saved. Correcting legislation that lifts the restraints of freedom of speech, freedom of thought and freedom of religion is the only way the word of God will be allowed to be heard.

References

[1] *Racial Discrimination Act 1975* /Australian Government.

[2] *Ibid.*

[3] Joe Ford, What is the old saying sticks and stones may break my bones? April 25, 2021, answerstoall.com.

[4] *The Sex Discrimination Act 1984* /Australian Government.

[5] Amelia Gentleman, The Great Nursery Debate, October 2, 2021. *The Guardian.*

6. *Sex Discrimination Amendment* (Sexual Orientation, Gender Identity, and Intersex Status) *Act 2013* / Australian Government

7. Marina Watts, Barbara Walters Accuses Corey Feldman of 'Damaging Entire Industry' with Paedophilia Accusation, August 14, 2021, *Newsweek.*

8. PlaySchool (2004) - Two Mums, Vimeo.

9. Safe Schools Coalition Aus. http://www.safeschoolscoalition.org.au/

10. *The Good Society; A respect matters education resource*/ Australian Government Department of Education, 2021.

11. Jack Phillips, Wikipedia Co-founder Warns: 'Wikipedia Is More One-Sided Than Ever', July 5, 2021, *The Epoch Times.*

12. *Ibid.*

13. Diego German Gonzalez, The Telegraph vs. Wikipedia. He qualifies it as "wokepedia", May 27, 2021. linuxadictos.com.

14. Ibid.

15. Ibid.

16. Internet Archive Wayback Machine. https://archive.org/web/

17. Alegra Hall, Mark Martin, Donna Russell, Christian Posts Blocked: Will 'Christian Speech' Be Allowed in the New Facebook World? October 10, 2018. CBS NEWS.

Rev Hon Fred Nile MLC is the longest serving elected member of NSW Parliament's Upper House and he is President of the Christian Democratic Party (CDP).

8
Where to from here?

Lyle Shelton

"Truth, Beauty and Goodness can be found and brought to life again, though doing so will cost you nothing less than everything." – Rod Dreher[1]

We are at a unique moment in Australian history. In 2017, most of the church sat on the sidelines of what will likely go down as the most consequential social policy battle of our generation. The loss of the definition of marriage in law now authorises the final de-legitimisation of the claims of Christianity in the modern world.

As the Roman Catholic Archbishop of Philadelphia in the United States, Charles Chaput points out in his book, *Strangers in a Strange Land*, Christians have gone from pillars to pariahs in just 20 years.[2] While some of this is self-inflicted because of despicable child sexual abuse and cover-up within the church's own ranks, much of it has been driven by a broader animus amongst secular elites towards Christianity and its public truth claims.

Wednesday 15 November 2017 was the day the Australian Bureau of Statistics announced the result of the Australian Marriage Law Postal Survey. Australians voted to redefine marriage by 62 per cent to 38 per cent. As this sunk in in the immediate hours afterwards my heart was filled with a sense of grief over the failure of much of the leadership of the church in Australia to speak. I remain convinced that losing marriage was avoidable.

Confirming our pillar to pariah status, the Australian Parliament proceeded swiftly and emphatically to reject amendments to the same-sex marriage legislation which would have protected freedom of speech, conscience, and religion. That several senior members of the Liberal Party and one from the National Party, the parties which have traditionally boasted they are the parties of freedom, joined with Labor and the Greens to vote against upholding freedom of speech, conscience and religion shows that we are in unchartered waters as a nation.

Let that sink in. The Australian Parliament has now created a situation where someone speaking out loud about their belief that marriage is exclusively between one man and one woman is vulnerable to be taken to a state-based anti-discrimination commission and fined. At the time of writing the Morrison Government was seeking to make good on an election promise to protect religious freedom through a Religious Discrimination Bill. While it may do some good, it is unlikely that that bill will restore what has been lost.

This is not the Australia I grew up in and it is not the Australia so many No voting migrants fled to from regimes which do not allow civic freedom. The ability of Christian schools to teach children the truth about marriage and gender remains uncertain more than two years after the postal plebiscite. Even what pastors preach about marriage and Biblical sexuality is vulnerable to legal action. Many have already been self-censoring. I know of a pastor who preached a series on the Bible's view of homosexuality. It was gracious and not in any way bigoted towards gay people. Like any sexual activity outside of heterosexual marriage, the Bible teaches that homosexuality is sin. Yet identity politics will not tolerate anything other than the celebration of homosexuality in today's society. This sermon series was the only series that he did not put on the internet for people to download for fear of being misrepresented as a hater and a bigot. I listened to the series. Sure, there is gentle disagreement over sexual morality, but that doesn't equate to hatred and there was none exhibited or incited by this pastor.

Are we going to be more or less free to speak about the Bible's vision for human sexuality and marriage now that marriage has been redefined in law and state-based anti-discrimination law weaponised? The answer is clearly less. What are we to do?

It seems to me that the church is responding to the crisis in two ways. One is to largely ignore what is happening in the culture and to keep preaching the Gospel of personal salvation and building local mega-churches, where possible. This vision assumes that we can largely ignore politics and culture. And besides, a Pentecostal Prime Minister is in the Lodge so everything should be fine. Right? But, in my view, once you are too afraid to post your sermons on-line or are self-censoring what is said from the pulpit, you are on a slippery slope to compromise and accommodation with the world.

How long do churches think they can sit outside politics before politics comes after them? A culture and body politic that rejects the idea of a Judge and therefore judgement of their actions, will come after any group in their society which publicly claims that humans are to be held to account by the Divine. This is what Christianity teaches, but that does not suit modern humankind who believe they are autonomous and accountable to no-one but themselves. In not speaking into politics and culture, how much of the church's witness of the Gospel must become private before the Gospel cannot be preached at all?

The second approach is to try and appeal to the world through loving unconditionally and without judgement, in the hope this will win people to Jesus. This is embodied in Baptist Minister Michael Frost's criticism of the Coalition for Marriage's campaign during the 2017 marriage postal survey. The following was published on the Bible Society-owned Eternity News website in the aftermath of the campaign. Frost said: *"Advertisements made by the Coalition for Marriage, in my view were scare-mongering with stories about kids wearing opposite sex clothing to school and questioning the legitimacy of non-traditional families. There seemed to be no sensitivity to how these kinds of changes would be felt by those who don't or can't fit into traditional family arrangements."*

He went on to say: *"Now is the time to redouble our efforts to love our neighbours, to seek to be Christ's representatives in the world."*[3] That last point is of course an important point and one that we were very much alive to even during the campaign.

But let's examine the overall implications of what is being implied. Why does Frost seem to assume that promoting a Biblical anthropology in public means that Christians do not love their neighbour? Is Frost saying that mothers' claims that their sons were told by "Safe Schools" that they could wear a dress to school were false? Is he saying the Coalition for Marriage was lying? Is he saying that Christians should not express concern about the injustice to children created by confusing them about their God-given gender or of legitimising non-Biblical family types?

Is he saying that if people don't fit into the traditional family type, they should feel free to use anonymous sperm donation and commercial surrogacy to cut-off children from their natural parents so they can create the type of family that suits them? Why was a Baptist minister saying this? Why was the Bible Society publishing this as a "Christian view?"

For mainstream Christianity throughout history, quietism and appeasement have often been attractive, but have never been the way. But both are attractive to some of the leading voices in the church in Australia right now. And that is understandable because the cultural and political environment is tough.

In my view, quietism is misguided and assumes we can get on with our lives as Christians by somehow sailing under the radar. But it is not business as usual anymore for Biblical Christians. What I call appeasement – and that might be a bit harsh because the motivation is to love people in the hope of not creating obstacles to Jesus – is also untenable. It assumes, wittingly or unwittingly, that somehow *shalom* can be achieved without offending our neighbours.

Of course, our motivation should never be to offend for the sake of it. We should always strive to be gracious, to speak the truth in love. But appeasement forgets that Jesus was a "rock of offense", and that the Gospel is often offensive to people. Both quietism and appeasement assume that the Gospel need not apply beyond personal salvation and works of charity, both of which of course are non-negotiable to Christianity.

But by themselves, these approaches are untenable in the current political and social environment. This is because I believe Christians have always been called to present the truth claims of Christ and his Word to the world *in public* and without fear.

Christian philosopher and apologist Os Guinness's 2016 book is entitled *Impossible People, the struggle for the soul of civilisation*. Most Christians are oblivious to the idea that there is even a struggle for the soul of western civilisation. We don't even realise that this struggle is about expunging the last vestiges of Christianity from our culture. Guinness says: *"Today's challenge rivals that of the fateful clash of the early church with the Caesars in the first three centuries* and the menace of the sultans of Ottoman Islam in the sixteenth."[4]

If the church really believed this, would so much of it have sat out the recent campaign to preserve marriage and the numerous other important cultural debates that have been playing out in our parliaments in recent years?

Before we get too pessimistic, we must remember that the church responded to and outlasted both of those earlier threats – the Romans and the Ottomans - and will outlast the present challenges. But, like rabbits in the headlights, we are still trying to figure out how to respond to our current crisis.

As I mentioned earlier, the same-sex marriage debate was a proxy for a much bigger prize. Prime Minister John Howard knew this. He told the graduates of the Catholic liberal arts college, Campion College, in 2011: *"Changing the definition of marriage, which has lasted for time immemorial, is not an exercise in human rights and equality; it is an exercise in de-authorising the Judeo-Christian influence in our society, and any who pretend otherwise are deluding themselves."*[5] And that is exactly what happened in December 2017 when the Parliament rejected the idea that those who will always believe the truth about marriage should be allowed to say this in public without risk of being fined.

But of course, a cultural crisis is only symptomatic of the underlying spiritual crisis.

Pope Emeritus Benedict XVI said: *"The spiritual crisis in the West is the most serious since the fall of the Roman Empire in the 5th Century."*[6] This is a big claim, but it is true.

Fr Martin, a modern-day Benedictine Monk says: *"When the light in most peoples' faces comes from the glow of a laptop, smartphone or television screen, we are living in a new Dark Age."*[7]

This leads me to the much-talked about book *The Benedict Option*

– A Strategy for Christians in a Post-Christian Nation. Rod Dreher's thesis is worth exploring. Dreher contends that we should "stop fighting the flood." Stop fighting political battles that are unwinnable. Having just spent 20 years of my life fighting the flood with my finger in the dyke and in this current moment of fatigue, I am attracted momentarily to what Dreher is saying.

He says we should build an ark and wait until the waters recede. We should take a leaf out of the Benedictine monastic movement's playbook – the Rule of Saint Benedict which Dreher says was "a monastic guidebook that played a powerful role in preserving Christian culture throughout the so-called Dark Ages".

St Benedict arose in the 6th century after the collapse of the Roman Empire which had been Christianised by Constantine, before being overrun by the barbarians. The Rule meant hunkering down into a life of prayer, work and reading the scriptures. Not enough Christians today prioritise prayer and reading the scriptures.

The Rule means a return to asceticism where we master our bodily desires for physical pleasure and materialistic pursuits in favour of spiritual growth. This is all relevant advice to us modern Christians who love our materialistic pleasures. We should withdraw and rebuild our communities of faith and especially cultivate Christian and home schooling to form the new generation, he advises.

In reading *The Benedict Option* I realised that the church and Christian school community I grew up in was forty years ahead of Rod Dreher. My father, Ian Shelton, who had a radical conversion to Christ as a teenager having grown up in a spiritually dead Methodist Church in country Queensland, intuitively new these things. From the mid-1970s, his church majored on prayer, Bible, the spiritual disciplines, building strong families and Christian community. Recognising the culture was turning against us and our families, he started a Christian school in 1979. I grew up living the Benedict Option.

But we always knew all these good things were not enough in the face of an increasingly hostile culture. And I think Dreher intuitively knows this too, because he does say, despite his assertion that we should not fight unwinnable political battles, that we *should* continue to be a prophetic voice into politics. Being a prophetic voice inevitably means tilting at windmills, as we proclaim truth to power when it does not wish to hear it.

And again, seemingly undermining his thesis, Dreher quotes from the great Czech playwright, resistance leader and political prisoner Vaclav Havel. Havel's 1978 essay "The Power of the Powerless" electrified Eastern European resistance movements.

Havel said that if we "live within the lie" we collaborate with the system – in his case the atheistic communist system – and we compromise our full humanity.[8]

I was heartened to read this in the Benedict Option and even more heartened by being privileged to hear Dreher speak in Brisbane in 2019 and have a brief conversation with him at a private dinner afterwards. He is certainly not advocating withdrawal in the way that perhaps some have sought to interpret him.

When a Baptist minister like Michael Frost casts doubt on warnings children will be taught that their gender is not based on their God-given biology, he is compromising our humanity which is based on the *imago Dei*. Male and female he created them in his image. When the Bible Society gives a platform to such compromise of our full humanity, it throws Biblical anthropology under the bus. It becomes complicit in the lie.

Where I think Frost and the Bible Society get muddled is in

their genuine desire to love our neighbour, they think we should not speak truth to our neighbour for fear of causing offense and putting up a blocker to the gospel. They perhaps think Christian political activism is about power and lording it over people – asserting some sort of God-given propriety right in society. I don't believe that at all. I believe we are to emulate the humble King who rode into Jerusalem on a donkey, but who was also bold in speaking truth to power as he did to Rome's Pontius Pilate and the powerful religious leaders of his day. We don't love our neighbours by giving succour to cultural lies which cause harm to the most vulnerable.

Dreher goes on to say that we are not looking to create heaven on earth. But if that is true, then Jesus died and rose from the dead in vain. What was the Lord's prayer all about? In it Jesus asks us to pray that heaven will come to earth. Sounds like a good prayer when there is so much hell on earth. Instead of bringing heaven to earth, too many Christians are focussed on getting out of earth to heaven.

Why did Jesus command his disciples to go and make disciples of all nations? To win souls, yes. But that is just the start. The Bible teaches that salvation is the rule of the King, Jesus. Over everything. It is much bigger than personal piety, as important and necessary as that is.

We are not meant to live in a monastery until Jesus comes back and raptures us out of a burning world going to hell. In fairness to Dreher that is not what he is meaning, but there is enough ambiguity in what he is saying to give comfort to those who would withdraw from the hard cultural and political fights of our day. Remember, most Christians are looking for such a permission structure to lay low – having just sat out of the biggest cultural battle of our generation.

The other important Christian cultural book of 2017 was *Strangers in a Strange Land – Living the Catholic Faith in a Post-Christian World* by Charles Chaput. Like Dreher, Chaput gives the same sober analysis of our current political and cultural environment. But rather than retreat, or give a permission structure for retreat, Chaput reminds us that Jesus left us with a mandate to transform creation. Chaput says: "The Gospel should move us to change the world for the better, not to bless it as it is."[9] The Bible tells us that Jesus is ruling and reigning even now and Chaput says we are called to work for that reign of Christ.[10]

One of the verses in the Christmas carol Joy to the World starts with: "He rules the world with truth and grace..." This has been the belief and assertion of Christianity to the world for two millennia. It has always made Christians unpopular because we say there is another King, and it is not Caesar.

We respect Caesar and the governing authorities – the Bible is clear on that. But our allegiance is foremost to the true King, and we seek to see his peace and reign fill the earth. Christ's kingdom comes because God builds it with our hands, Chaput says.[11] We don't fight for it with swords, as Jesus' disciples sought to when he was arrested in the Garden of Gethsemane. It is a kingdom that is built not by the ways of Machiavelli but through grace, love, and servant leadership. As Chaput rightly points out, the church is resented because it calls faithful people to act. The world would prefer we didn't and many Christians, comfortable in the four walls of their church buildings, are sadly okay with that.

We saw that resentment on display when the plebiscite and the Parliament took away our legal right to act to promote publicly Christ's design for marriage and family. Whether most of our fellow Australians and our elected representatives did this willingly or unwittingly, under law, that is what they have effectively done.

There was nothing unwitting, though, about the intentions of the rainbow political activists to whom our politicians capitulated. Our view of marriage and family has now been cast aside in law, having already been cast aside through the sexual revolution of the 1960s. We are indeed strangers in a strange land. Mordor is coming for the Hobbits in the Shire.

Chaput also says, despite this, that the task to which God calls us is to hold the world together. And this brings me to what I call the "indispensable people".

The American founders, from whom the Australian founders borrowed so much, knew that freedom and democracy would not work unless there was virtue amongst the general population.

"Can the liberties of a nation be thought secure when we have removed their only firm basis, a conviction in the minds of the people, that these liberties are the gift of God?" said Thomas Jefferson.[12] *"Our Constitution was made only for a moral and religious people. It is wholly inadequate to the government of any other,"* asserted John Adams.[13] *"Before any man can be considered a member of civil society, he must be considered as a subject of the governor of the universe,"* proclaimed James Madison.[14]

These were the people who invented modern democracy and freedom as a political system. They knew that without virtue which comes from Christian faith, there would be no political freedom. This is what Guinness calls the Golden Triangle of Freedom.

While most of the American founders were Christians and all were subscribers to a Christian worldview, they were also tolerant of those who were not. "Government has no Right to hurt a hair of the head of an atheist for his opinions," said John Adams.[15]

Imagine if our human rights commissions had this much tolerance towards Christians who had different opinions to those of rainbow orthodoxy? But importantly, Adams' tolerance which I know is shared by most Christians today, means our non-Christian friends have nothing to fear from us.

The Frenchman, Alexis de Tocqueville, who famously went to investigate what was going on in this new experiment in democracy in the United States wrote in Democracy in America: "Christianity must be maintained at any cost in the bosom of modern democracies."[16]

Today the idea of Christianity being indispensable to political freedom and democracy is scoffed at. The reality is that Christians have been and will continue to be "indispensable people" in a society that has lost its moorings.

But it was not just the Americans who saw the importance of the role of Christianity. Our greatest Prime Minister, Sir Robert Menzies, recognised the threat of totalitarian Communism to liberty as it gathered momentum in the wake of World War II. He said Communism *"can have nothing but hostility towards religion and in particular the Christian faith"*.[17] I wonder what Menzies would make of today's Left in Australia and their hostility towards Christianity.

Menzies also knew that the Christian ideal of marriage and family was vital to civil society and should be defended. "If you secure a copy of the Communist Manifesto and look at chapter 2 you will see how it embraces the abolition of the family; the abolition of what is called bourgeois marriage; the abolition of country and nationality."[18] If Menzies were alive today, he would have the good sense to recognise the same threat but instead of under a red flag, under a rainbow flag. This is why it was ludicrous for senior Liberals like the party's President, Nick Greiner, to assert during the marriage debate that Menzies would have supported redefining marriage.[19] Menzies was famous for his "Forgotten People" radio broadcasts, but it is amazing how quickly his own have forgotten what he really stood for.

In another of his Forgotten People radio broadcasts, Menzies was open about his Presbyterian faith. "The most important thing in the world, may I say for myself, is man's relation to his maker: his relation to the divine and spiritual law. The second most important thing is man's relation to man."[20]

Menzies knew the importance of faith, family, and freedom to the health of the nation. It has been a long time since a modern Liberal articulated the importance of these with such Menzian clarity.

But not everything was perfect in Menzies' 1950s. Just like today, the church had its problems. But it is fascinating that Menzies, as Prime Minister, took it upon himself to upbraid elements of the church for sailing towards the siren song of communism. "There is nothing more astonishing than the success with which revolutionary communism has wooed and won the support of not a few ardent Christians and churchgoers, including some in the clergy," Menzies chided.[21] Again, if he were alive today, he would make the same admonition of a small group of churches and Christian leaders who have embraced the rainbow flag. These, like Frost, bring confusion and undermine efforts to expose the injustices that fly under the rainbow flag.

Further evidence of the indispensable civilising capacity of Christianity is documented in political philosopher Larry Siedentop's book *Inventing the Individual, The Origins of Western Liberalism*. Education, the status of women, civic order, the idea that government should be by consent of the governed, the need for a society where people are governed by individual morality rather than brute force, all came from Christianity, according to Siedentop. His work is a remarkable tracking of the rise of western civilisation from pre-Roman paganism to the modern democratic nation state based on the rule of law and how Christianity influenced and drove every step of that journey.

Sadly, we are descending back into paganism and an inability to self-govern. Siedentop demonstrates how Christians began their march through the institutions, not through the use of worldly power, but by laying their lives down, like Jesus did.

The cult of Christian martyrs, choosing to obey God rather than civic authority, redefined heroism in the ancient world. Siedentop says, "the ancient hero was typically male, strong, wily and successful".[22] Think Zeus, think Thor, think Chris Hemsworth. "By contrast," Siedentop says, "the Christian martyr – whether facing stoning by a crowd, ferocious animals in a crowded stadium or burning on a pyre – was defying society".[23] Their blood, as Tertullian famously said, was the seed of the church.

Os Guinness's book *Impossible People* takes its title from the example of an 11th century Benedictine reformer by the name of Peter Damian, who became known as the "impossible man". A predecessor to Saint Francis of Assisi, Damian called for reform of Simony – the selling of church positions for money – he condemned the widespread acceptance of homosexuality, paedophilia, and pederasty, especially among the clergy. One thousand years later it would seem not much has changed.

To use a term coined by George Orwell, Guinness says Damian was "unclubbable" – he could not be co-opted into the *club* by ditching his principles. He did not feel the need to be one of the cool kids.

Guinness says too many Christians are caving in weakly before the challenges of our times such as the seductions and distortions of modernity, the temptations of the sexual revolution and a failure to appreciate the implacable hostility of the forces against us.

He goes on to say: *"All who would be faithful followers of Jesus in our advanced modern world are facing similar challenges and seductions, and we too must become impossible people – Christians with hearts that can melt with compassion, but with faces like flint and backbones of steel who are unmanipulable, unbiddable, undeterrable and unclubbable, without ever losing the gentleness, the mercy, the grace and compassion of our Lord."*[24]

Where are the Christians today who will stand against error and call out weakness in the church? Where are the people who will call out the injustices of public policy which deface the Imago Dei? And when told to be quiet or even to recant will echo Luther and say: "I cannot do otherwise. Here I stand. God help me. Amen."? Where are those who, like the martyrs of old, will defy society?

I'll give the last word to Rod Dreher. *"Truth, Beauty and Goodness can be found and brought to life again, though doing so will cost you nothing less than everything."*[25] There is a big task in front of us. My prayer is that Australia's Christians and their churches will be willing to pay the price.

References

[1] Dreher, Rod; *The Benedict Option – A Strategy for Christians in a Post-Christian Nation;* Sentinel; New York; 2017; p. 77.

[2] Chaput, Archbishop Charles; *Strangers in a Strange Land;* Henry Holt and Company; 2017; p. 3.

[3] Frost, Michael; Admit it, YES 'romped it in'; *Eternity News;* Bible Society

of Australia; November 29, 2017.

4 Guinness, Os, *Impossible People – Christian Courage and the Struggle for the Soul of Civilisation;* InterVarsity Press; 2016; pp. 23-24.

5 van Gend, David; Conscience demands we debate moral issues unimpeded; *The Australian;* December 26, 2015.

6 Dreher, Rod; *Op. cit.;* p. 8.

7 *Ibid.;* p. 71

8 *Ibid.;* p. 92.

9 Chaput, Archbishop Charles; *Strangers in a Strange Land;* Henry Holt and Company; 2017; p. 78.

10 *Ibid.;* p. 161.

11 *Ibid.*

12 Neuhaus, Richard John; *The Naked Public Square: Religion and Democracy in America;* William B. Eerdmans Publishing Company; Grand Rapids, Michigan; 1997; p. 100.

13 George, Robert P.; Could America Survive without Religion? *The Public Discourse;* November 19, 2015.

14 Madison, James; *Memorial and Remonstrance Against Religious Assessments;* 1785.

15 Hutson, James H; *The Founders on Religion: A Book of Quotations;* Princeton University Press; Princeton; 2005.

16 Tocqueville, Alexis De; *Democracy in America.*

17 Communism and Christianity Broadcast, 1946; *Menzies – the Forgotten Speeches;* edited by David Furse Roberts; Connor Court Publishing; 2017, p. 233.

18 *Ibid.;* p. 231.

19 Greiner, Nick; Marriage for all: a conservative ideal; *The Australian;* August 28, 2017.

20 Education and Moral Character broadcast 1954; *Menzies – the Forgotten*

Speeches; edited by David Furse Roberts; Connor Court Publishing; 2017; p. 264.

21 Communism and Christianity Broadcast, 1946; M*enzies – the Forgotten Speeches*, edited by David Furse Roberts; Connor Court Publishing; 2017; p. 229.

22 Siedentop, Larry; *Inventing the Individual – The Origins of Western Liberalism;* The Belknap Press of Harvard University Press, Cambridge Massachusetts; 2014; p. 79.

23 *Ibid.*

24 Guinness, Os; *Impossible People – Christian Courage and the Struggle for the Soul of Civilisation;* InterVarsity Press; 2016.

25 Dreher, Rod; *Op cit;* p. 77.

Lyle Shelton was the former Managing Director of Australian Christian Lobby. This chapter first appeared in the book *I Kid You Not – Notes From 20 Years in the Trenches of the Culture Wars* (Connor Court, 2020). It is reprinted with the permission of Connor Court Publishing

9

"The Time for Alibis and Excuses Has Expired" - Religious Freedoms and Parental Rights in the Age of Cancel Culture

Hon Mark Latham MLC

Introduction

Twenty years ago, I argued that Australia's social contract was in need of revitalisation, and that focusing on *mutualism* – the organic relationship between people and their non-hierarchical reciprocal bonds of interpersonal trust – could help rebuild lost social capital.[1] It is difficult not to conclude that things have only gotten worse. In the years that have passed, we have witnessed the concentration of power into a faceless and unaccountable state bureaucracy, the promotion of a "woke" ideology in education, and the proliferation of a toxic culture of aggressive activism that continues to undermine our civil society. All these trends have weakened our social capital, while the rights of individuals have been routinely discarded and traditional norms abandoned. A recent State Curriculum Review has admitted that the role of schools is to usurp the traditional parental privilege of inculcating values, developing character and providing stewardship over the emotional and social development of the young.[2] Indeed, where the educational system was once predicated on the application of discipline in training and education, now it is little more than a perpetual revolution where all values are erased or deconstructed into oblivion.³ Likewise, as the persecution of public figures such as Israel Folau and Margaret Court has shown in recent years, people of faith are increasingly being relegated to second class status in the public square.⁴ What is going on, and what can be done to alleviate this lamentable state of affairs?

Cancel Culture and the New 'Tolerance'

In the not too recent past, conservative commentators such as Nick Cater would castigate disingenuous and out-of-touch public intellectuals for promoting a culture of self-loathing.⁵ Deconstructive "black armband" views of history and culture would be imposed top-down. In recent years, however, the cancer has metastasised into something much more insidious. Far-Left views of social policy have come to aggressively dominate social discourse, creating an atmosphere of fear, and making frank and honest debate impossible. As former Australian High Court Justice Dyson Heydon has said, "it is all right for the elite to support a particular point of view, but intolerable for anyone else to oppose it. That is what modern elites call 'tolerance'."⁶ Today, an activist class of "social justice warriors" has taken what was once an elite driven top-down approach of social engineering and turned it into an ideological virus that has polarised society and resulted in deplatforming, ostracisation, and the ruination of people's careers and lives, simply for views they hold on to matters of faith and family. Katherine Kersten writes in *First Things* that: "Few citizens dare to disagree publicly, which is no surprise. Attacks on dissenters in the press and social media have been ruthless, and some of the targets have lost their reputations and livelihoods."⁷

This culture of coercion and fear is drawn from the "repressive tolerance" theories of the Frankfurt School, which taught that ideas and views deemed offensive to self-declared social reformers must be treated with contempt and removed from the public square. History has shown that controlling the very language that people use results in the control of ideas and thoughts expressed in public.[8] In turn, the cancellation of ideas leads to the cancellation of the people who express them. Independent journalist Andy Ngo is a notable example. He was viciously assaulted by an "antifascist" gang while filing a report at one of the riots that peppered the US in the last months of the Trump presidency.[9] This was only to be expected given the ideological foundations of the far left's agitators. One of the Frankfurt School's leading thinkers, Herbert Marcuse, openly advocated for the use of violence by an "oppressed" people because, as he argued, to condemn *all* violence equally would only reinforce existing structures of social authority.[10] Instead of pursuing equity and fairness, this ideology seeks to undermine, attack, and demolish traditional values and social structures which once nourished a community and provided it with a civilising framework. Thus, Paul Gottfried refers to "critical race theory" – another fashionable catchphrase of the activist class – as an "inversion of patriotic myths" which is "about laying guilt trips on those whom our elites seek to control" in an "effort to reconstruct people's minds and to make them responsive to an expanded leftist agenda."[11]

Progressive social engineers know that their efforts to rebuild society according to utopian blueprints are futile without first delegitimising traditional notions of family, the moral ethos it is based on, and reducing its defenders to second class citizens in the public square. Consider the example of "Black Lives Matter" which declared an interest in "disrupting the Western-prescribed nuclear family structure requirement."[12] Existing loyalties and beliefs must be dismantled across the board. Whether it's CRT, BLM or the redefinition of marriage, these causes cannot be properly understood in isolation from each other because all of them fall under the banner of post-modern deconstruction.

Religious Freedoms and Parental Rights

An echo of Marcuse's theories of "repressive tolerance" has unsurprisingly made its presence felt where religious freedoms are at stake: not all people seem to be protected in anti-discrimination laws because not all rights are equal in the eyes of the law. When I introduced my Bill to protect religious liberties in May 2020,[13] I noted some examples of modern-day persecution and rights-denial for which there is no legal redress. Many of these examples occurred during the campaign to legalise same-sex marriage and demonstrate a clear conflict of rights situation for which there is no effective mechanism for mediation. Consider the following:

- A wedding magazine had to cease publication due to third party advertising boycotts simply because the owners ran their business according to traditional notions of family.[14]
- A brewing company was the subject of a vilification campaign for merely sponsoring a debate about proposals to redefine marriage.[15]
- A business executive was forced to resign from the board of a Christian advocacy group because of a similar activist campaign.[16]
- An academic was sacked from his position at a university due to being a director of a Christian training institute.[17]
- Christian medical practitioners have also been stripped of their accreditation for refusing to surrender to the demands of gender ideology.[18]

This is just a representative sample. More recently, the advent of Dominic Perrottet as New South Wales Premier was met with old fashioned sectarianism from the Left. After a series of NSW Premiers of Catholic faith with large families in state history, in 2021 it was deemed peculiar that a Catholic with 6 children would lead our state. Perrottet was hung out as a public spectacle to be mocked by the ABC, the Greens, and other Leftist cadres.

I have been approached by incredulous constituents who cannot believe that they immigrated to Australia with the hope of escaping religious discrimination, only to find it spreading here as well. The Bible has been the source for a moral code that both religious and secular citizens appeal to when they speak of human dignity, freedom, respect, and equity. Religious freedoms are no fringe issue but lie at the heart of civil society. Yet while every letter of the alphabet has its own legislated protection, those who subscribe to Christian moral norms are left out of the diversity paradigm altogether. Defenders of religious liberty correctly point out that faith "inspires people to think beyond the narrow confines of their own lives and daily tribulations to encompass a wider perspective."[19] In contrast, the closed mind does not create a more tolerant and inclusive society, but rather a one marked by an "absence of curiosity."[20] It is therefore no surprise that those who complain the loudest about the supposed ignorance of the traditionally-minded are themselves remarkably ignorant.

There has been a need for a Bill to protect religious liberties since at least the Wran Government in 1977, when the first anti-discrimination legislation was passed in this state.[21] In 1988, the State Law Reform Commission recommended including religion as a ground of discrimination.[22] More recently, the Commonwealth review in to religious liberties echoed the same recommendation.[23] Yet, while the government had no compunction to expedite the liberalisation of abortion laws in the face of substantial community distress in 2019, no action has been taken to protect the human rights of faith communities, despite a clear public mandate and repeated recommendations from the most prestigious institutions of law reform.[24]

The bureaucratic encroachment on the rights of parents is another area where traditional liberties have been whittled away. This has occurred where controversial ideologies are inserted into classrooms, such as gender fluidity and other radical political causes, without the knowledge, or despite parental consent. Many of these agendas likewise offend the religious and cultural sensibilities of a substantial cross-section of society. The government has stated on various occasions that the so-called "Safe Schools" programme does not form part of the educational curriculum in our schools. The programme was promoted by Roz Ward of La Trobe University, who argued in 2014 that the "Safe Schools Coalition is about supporting gender and sexual diversity. It's not about celebrating diversity. It's not about stopping bullying. It's about gender and sexual diversity. It's about same sex attraction. It's about being transgender."[25] One year later Ward went on the record saying that "Marxism offers the hope and the strategy needed to create a world where human sexuality, gender and how we relate to our bodies can blossom in extraordinarily new and amazing ways that we can only try to imagine today."[26] As I pointed out to Parliament when introducing a Bill to reassert parental primacy in the law,[27] despite government assurances to the contrary the substance of this agenda continues to be pushed by politically driven educrats, albeit in rebranded and repackaged form.

The Teacher Learning Network has no less than 23 courses focusing on explicit political indoctrination in the areas of refugee policy, climate change, colonisation, and gender ideology. The universities are likewise infiltrated by this activism masquerading as scholarship. Western Sydney University is the worst offender with numerous "centres" dedicated to "research" on gender fluidity, and where Jackie Ullman, who promotes texts that encourage the teaching of gender ideology in classrooms[28] is currently working to undermine the government's supposed repealing of the "Safe Schools" agenda. Classroom practice manuals issued by the University of Newcastle instruct educators to encourage children in kindergarten to think of nuclear families as "problematic". Some Catholic institutions such as the St Mary Star of the Sea Catholic College in Wollongong have formally "degendered" language, and its year 11 geography classes feature material on "misgendered babies". A course offered by "MultiVerse" encourages educators to "put on their queer lens" when teaching children as young as three, while a textbook promoted by Red Ruby Scarlett instructs teachers to "challenge gender and sexuality stereotypes."[29] Material leaked from private social media communities has shown her running seminars online at which teachers are instructed how to incorporate transgendered characters into teaching material.

Despite statements by the education minister that "encouraging positions on social and political issues is not the job of schools"[30] those within her department obviously aren't listening. The government has clearly lost control of their own bureaucracy, which runs the educational system and has found ways to continue abusing it as a vehicle of social and political change, instead of focusing on its fundamental purpose: to provide the kind of education for young Australians that will allow them to have the best start in life. Unsurprisingly, the environment in which teachers are trained is anarchic. In the 2020 State Education Standards Authority noted the existence of 42,000 accredited teacher professional courses.[31] There is no centralised quality control supervision. Auditing this number of materials is estimated to take a decade. This is a perfect environment in which nefarious agendas can be camouflaged in the jungle of administrative and bureaucratic chaos that marks the state of education in New South Wales. It is no surprise therefore that

"Safe Schools" styled agendas continue to thrive even while the Minister for Education repeatedly declares such programmes rescinded.

The usurpation of parental rights by the educational bureaucracy is akin to the psychological colonisation of the minds of children. Social engineers believe themselves better suited to shape the ethical and moral framework of future generations. By pushing toxic ideologies onto the most vulnerable persons in our community, some as young as three, five or six years of age, they violate one of the core principles of pedagogy, which is to *do no harm*. The programmes illustrated above turn classrooms into political indoctrination camps where children are sexualised through gender fluidity advocacy, and which will undoubtedly lead to confusion, anxiety, and mental illness.

A Solution

Under present conditions, a practical solution to this problem will involve legislating protections that cover the field. This will have a dual effect of guaranteeing rights that have been eroded over the years by managerial elite, and hopefully also contribute to the push-back against cancel culture in the public square.

The Religious Freedoms and Equality Bill extends protection from discrimination to people of religious faith by enshrining the *Universal Declaration of Human Rights*, which clearly identifies religious freedom as a right that every person should be able to exercise collectively or individually, in private or in public.[32] Furthermore, the Bill seeks to arrest the corporate suppression of workers' rights to express their faith. It will therefore incorporate the basic principles of international human rights law. This will be achieved by defining "religious belief" as a sincerely held conviction, opinion, or affiliation, while "discrimination" will be defined simply as less favourable treatment of a targeted individual, or his or her associate – religious observance will thus become an attribute protected under State discrimination law. Religious ethos organisations will be exempt, so that they may continue to operate in accordance with their doctrines, tenets, beliefs, and teachings. Incorporating the spirit of General Comment 18 of the UN Human Rights Committee,[33] absurd legal findings will be avoided, such as the one that held the St Vincent de Paul society as not a "body established for religious purposes."[34] Where conflicts of rights occur, the Syracuse Principles' test of proportionally will be incorporated as a mediating strategy, one which has a track record of successful application overseas.[35]

The penultimate objective of the Parental Rights Bill is to outlaw gender ideology indoctrination in New South Wales schools, remove it from course development and teacher training, as well as reassert the rights of parents in the education of their children's moral, ethical and social development. By explicitly introducing "matters of parental primacy" into State law, this Bill enshrines the provisions of Article 18(4) of the *International Covenant on Civil and Political Rights,* namely the "respect for the liberty of parents [...] to ensure the religious and moral education of their children in conformity with their own convictions." These matters will remain the province of parental decision making, well outside the jurisdiction of a politicised bureaucracy, teachers unions and the agenda driven activist class.[36] The Bill itself was the subject of a Committee of Inquiry to which the public was invited to make submissions. An overwhelming majority of these were favourable. Three quarters stated that parents don't have enough say in what their children are taught in school, 88% wanted to be provided with an extensive outline of the curriculum before it is implemented and 79% demanded a right to withdraw their children from class if the material offends their cultural and moral sensibilities. Over half supported the Bill in its present, unamended form.[37]

Both Bills, once passed, would significantly improve the health of our civil society. They are reasonable in their scope and application. The community wants the protections they offer. The only thing missing is the political leadership necessary within government to respond to this need.

A Return to Society Based on Reason and Respect

Richard Koch and Chris Smith have written that institutions could be seen as "frozen beliefs" because they embody an organisational framework for how a people lives and governs itself. Consider this key passage: "institutions were, and are, often unfrozen and refrozen in the West in accordance with new beliefs."[38] This evolution in institutions can only occur if the people who are served by them can openly and freely discus, debate, and interrogate new ideas, and properly investigate changes in their beliefs. No change can ever occur outside this paradigm of free expression. It is perhaps ironic that the "woke" advocates of "cancel culture" are therefore guaranteeing the death of any real prospect of social progress through their totalitarian programmes of thought control. Their alternative is a society where certain pre-approved ideas are unchallengeable, i.e., sacred. In other words, a society that is *fundamentalist* in what it views to be true. Should Australia go down this track, we have the precedent of the Unites States to illustrate where this will lead.

Today's cancel culture destroys interpersonal trust. It is the logical evolution of "repressive tolerance" into the modern era and a complete repudiation of the fundamental attitude on which

Western civilisation was built, namely, that ideas could and should be tested through rigorous debate and intellectual interrogation. The law presently fails to protect a vast majority of Australians who cannot express themselves for fear of mob reprisal. We need to return to the previous tradition of civil discourse and mutual respect. This can only be achieved by passing the legislative guarantees in the two Bills I have discussed here. I agree with Dominic Raab who writes in *Assault on Liberty* that "pervasive political correctness and counter-productive attempts to protect the sensitivities of minority or vulnerable groups should give way to more rigorous debate."[39] He continues: "The British tradition of liberty provides the individual citizen, religious communities and other minority groups with the freedom to follow their faith and convictions, consistent with a singular, secular law that protects both freedom of conscience and the wider public interest in a clear and consistent demarcation of public – including criminal – law."[40]

This is essentially an appeal to an older form of classical liberalism which respected the diversity of views within the public square. A return to this paradigm can now only be achieved by expanding the field of human rights protection to those groups that are now targeted through malicious ideological campaigns, and the mission-creep of overzealous administrative politburos. Intellectual plurality is a condition for the creation of a dynamic culture capable of fostering the kind of society that so many around the world vote with the feet to join today. This was once the kind of world in which we lived, and it worked. Only returning to the principles that animated the social life of that world will we be able to create a mechanism by which people and communities can be heard, and their grievances properly addressed. The alternative offered by "cancel culture" is a world of intentional blindness and ignorance, where aggrieved parties will find themselves increasingly feeling the pressure of disenfranchisement and the frustration that will naturally arise from that.

Conclusion

This is the civil rights struggle of our time, and it shouldn't be seen as the special cause of any political orientation. Even a social commentator associated with the progressive commentariat such as Waleed Aly can see that "cancel culture" is a problem for both the right and the left. In an essay for *The Monthly* Aly concludes that its "civil nihilism" actually "reflects a nihilism already well established in our public culture."[41] Pioneering post-war conservative intellectuals in the United States such as Peter Viereck likewise opposed the "conformism" and "thought control" of both wings of the political spectrum.[42] Viereck was then a vocal opponent of reactionary McCarthyism, but his criticisms today can apply equally to the McCarthyism of the contemporary left as it persecutes ordinary people for expressing entirely legal opinions that run afoul of fashionable orthodoxy, or whose religious values and lifestyles are deemed offensive to "woke" activists. This is in fact an issue that concerns us all, and all Australians of good faith who genuinely value the merits of free through and expression should be deeply concerned about it irrespective of their party affiliation.

When the Parental Rights Bill was introduced into Parliament in August 2020, it was heckled by Left-wingers who accused its backers of wanting to "ban books."[43] What an ironic interjection from an ideology with a track record of literally cancelling people for wrong think.[44] I've read the material that is being pushed onto our young. That material is not fit for the purpose of education. It is designed to shape the morality and identity of children by sidelining the role parents play in raising their sons and daughters. Opposing the proliferation of this is not "book burning." It is a *rational response* from people to whom the mental and emotional health of our children is a greater priority than the utopian projects of cultural radicals. While introducing the Religious Freedom Bill I stated that "the time for alibis and excuses has expired."[45] For far too long, governing elites have held the legitimate interests of a broad cross-section of Australians in contempt, failing to answer important questions and ignoring calls for reform. In truth, that time for alibis and excuses expired at least 20 years ago when I spoke about the need for mutualism in Australian society. This need has only gotten greater with the passage of years. I have remained consistent in my advocacy for the interests of mainstream Australians who continue to be challenged by social and economic turbulence, but who now must additionally face a new totalitarianism, one which prohibits them complaining about attempts at top-down deconstruction of social institutions like the family, the redefinition of language, and being told how they can and cannot worship in their faith.

Like a virus, the self-loathing elites of yesteryear have today spread their ideological contagion to a gullible SJW mob. This may have made the task to returning to a fair and rational based society all the more difficult, but it is also all the more pressing for people of good faith who care about the direction Australia has chosen for its future. We may not have had many victories in recent years, but the current trajectory is untenable, and that should at least hearten us as we continue to fight what is right and true.

References

[1] Mark Latham, "Mutualism: A Third Way for Australia" *Quadrant* Vol. 44(3) No. 364 (March 2000). This presentation was originally delivered

at the Mutualism National Conference hosted by the Australian Fabian Society and Mutuality Australia in Melbourne, November 2000.

2. Geoff Masters, *Nurturing Wonder, and Igniting Passion: Designs for a New School Curriculum – NSW Curriculum Review* (NSW Educational Standards Authority, April 2020) p. 4 para 3.

3. Christopher Murray, "ACRA Proposal will Turn Every Book into a Closed Book" *News Weekly* No. 3093 (29 May 2021) p. 11.

4. John Carroll, "The Tyranny of Opinion" *The Australian* (18 January 2020) p. 17.

5. Nick Cater, *The Lucky Culture: and the Rise of an Australian Ruling Class* (Sydney; NSW: Harper Collins, 2013). See Chapter 13 in which the author illustrates the hypocritically moralised rhetoric of the self-loathing elite.

6. Dyson Heydon, "The Tyranny of Relativism: Religious 'Toleration' in Modern Australia" *Annals Australasia* Vol. 128(9/10) (November 2017) p. 41. This presentation was originally delivered at the Australian Catholic University (Adelaide campus) on 17 October 2017 as the Inaugural PM Glynn Lecture on Religion, Law and Public Life.

7. Katherine Kersten, "Adversary Culture in 2020" *First Things* No. 310 (February 2021) p. 42.

8. For a recent discussion, see: Wanda Skowronska, "Fighting the Pronoun Police" *Annals Australasia* Vol 128(1) (January-February 2017), *passim*.

9. Andy Ngo, *Unmasked: Inside Antifa's Radical Plan to Destroy Democracy* (New York: USA; Hatchet Street, 2021). See Chapters 8 to 10. See also Ngo's address to the Hillsdale College National Leadership Seminar: "Antifa: History and Tactics" (Franklin, Tennessee; 26-27 April 2021).

10. Rolf Wiggershaus, *The Frankfurt School: its History, Theories, and Political Significants* Michael Robertson (trans.), (Cambridge: Massachusetts; MIT Press, 2007) p. 612.

11. Paul Gottfried, "Flawed Reasoning on CRT" *Chronicles* Vol. 45(9) (September 2021) p. 6. Furthermore, Edwin Dyga has identified that this project is essentially driven by a spirit of malice: "Self-Loathing: the Other Pandemic of 2020" *Quadrant* Vol. 64(12) No. 572 (December 2020),

specifically pp. 37-38.

12 Portfolio Committee No. 3: Education, NSW Legislative Council, *Education Legislation Amendment (Parental Rights) Bill 2020* Report No. 44 (September 2021) p. vii. The statement has since been removed from the BLM website, but an archived version of the page can still be accessed via a search on <web.archive.org> for <blacklivesmatter.com/what-we-believe>. The first archive "snapshot" of the website dated 2 December 2019 clearly shows this statement at paragraph 20.

13 Anti-Discrimination Amendment (Religious Freedoms and Equality) Bill 2020.

14 "Wedding magazine shuts after boycott over refusal to include same-sex marriages" *Evangelical Focus* (online) (23 November 2018) <evangelicalfocus.com> (accessed 11 October 2021).

15 Paige Cockburn, "Coopers Brewery distances itself from Bible Society's same-sex marriage video, faces backlash" *ABC News* (online) (14 March 2017) <abc.net.au> (accessed 11 October 2021).

16 Julian Porteous, "Corporate bullying threatens our freedom" *The Australian* (15 April 2017) p. 18.

17 Jeremy Sammut, "Beware the intolerant 'diversity' warriors targeting corporations" *Australian Financial Review* (3 April 2017) p. 39.

18 See for example: "Melbourne doctor speaks about Medical Board's attack" *Family Voice Australia* (online) (2 November 2020) <familyvoice.org.au> (accessed 11 October 2021).

19 Ian Harper, "Religion Matters for Faith, Hope and Love" *Really Dangerous Ideas* Gary Johns (ed.) (Ballan: Victoria; Connor Court, 2013) p. 40.

20 Editorial, "Experiments Against Reality" *The New Criterion* Vol 38(1) (September 2019) pp. 2-3.

21 Religion as a ground for discrimination was intended to be part of the *Anti-Discrimination Act 1977* (NSW) but was removed before the Bill was passed.

22 Recommendation No. 38, Michael Adams *et al., Review of the Anti-Discrimination Act 1977* Report No. 92 (NSW Law Reform Commission, 1999).

23. Recommendation No. 16, Philip Ruddock *et al.*, *Religious Freedom Review: Report of the Expert Panel* (Commonwealth Attorney General's Department, 2018).

24. The excuse of a potential conflict with the proposed Commonwealth Religious Discrimination Bill 2019 is a nonsense: its section 62(1) clearly states that "[t]his Act is not intended to exclude or limit the operation of a law of a state or territory to the extent that the law is capable of operating concurrently with this Act."

25. Roz Ward, Address to the National Symposium of the Safe Schools Coalition (Melbourne, 13 June 2014).

26. Roz Ward, Address to the 2015 Marxism Conference: "The Role of the Left in the Struggle for LGBTI Rights" ([location unknown], 24-27 March 2015). This information has since been removed from the Marxism Conference website where it appeared as an audio file; an archived version of the page dated 3 August 2015 (but not the audio) can still be accessed via a search on <web.archive.org>; the quote cited here has been sourced *via* <sydneytrads.com/2016/02/29/roz-ward/>.

27. Educational Legislation Amendment (Parental Rights) Bill 2020.

28. Such as: Jón Ingvar Kjaran and Helen Sauntson (eds.), *Schools as Queer Transformative Spaces: Global Narratives on Sexualities and Gender* (Oxford; UK: Routledge, 2021).

29. Elizabeth Dau, *The Anti-Bias Approach to Early Childhood Education* (Pearson Education Australia, 2001).

30. Sarah Mitchell, "Recognise that marks matter to stop 20-year educational slide" *Sydney Morning Herald* (7 December 2019) p. 33.

31. Education Standards Authority, Press Release: "Overhaul of Teacher Training" (29 November 2020) <educationstandards.nsw.edu.au> (accessed 14 October 2021).

32. Art. 18, United Nations, *Universal Declaration of Human Rights* (1948). Australia is one of the first 48 countries who voted for the Declaration on 10 December 1948.

33. Sec. 22M, Anti-Discrimination Amendment (Religious Freedoms and Equality) Bill 2020.

34 *Walsh v St Vincent de Paul Society Queensland (No. 2)* [2008] QADT 32.

35 *Ngole v University of Sheffield* [2019] EWCA Civ 1127.

36 Secs. 17A-17D, Educational Legislation Amendment (Parental Rights) Bill 2020.

37 Portfolio Committee No. 3: Education, NSW Legislative Council, *Education Legislation Amendment (Parental Rights) Bill 2020* Report No. 44 (September 2021) p. viii. For a detailed analysis, see the data for Questions 2-8 at pp. 68-76 *op. cit.*

38 Richard Koch and Chris Smith, *Suicide of the West* (London: UK; Continuum, 2006) p. 179.

39 Dominic Raab, *The Assault on Liberty: What Went Wrong With Rights* (London: UK; Fourth Estate, 2009) p. 212.

40 *Ibid.*

41 Waleed Aly, "Woke Politics and Power: How Liberalism's Blind Spot Let Cancel Culture Bloom" *The Monthly* (November 2020) p. 35.

42 Peter Viereck, *The Unadjusted Man* (Westport: Connecticut; Greenwood Press, 1973 [1956]), Chapter 18 *passim.*

43 New South Wales, *Parliamentary Debates,* Legislative Council, 5 August 2020 (Mark Latham) (Second Reading Speech for the Educational Legislation Amendment (Parental Rights) Bill 2020) para. 15.

44 Jonathan van Maren, "The Witch Hunt Against Conservative Women" *The European Conservative* No. 20 (Fall, 2021), *passim.*

45 New South Wales, *Parliamentary Debates,* Legislative Council, 13 May 2020 (Mark Latham) (Second Reading Speech for the Anti-Discrimination Amendment (Religious Freedoms and Equality) Bill 2020) para. 19.

Hon Mark Latham MLC is leader of One Nation party in New South Wales since November 2018 and was elected to the Legislative Council in the 2019 state election.

10
Living Under a New Paradigm

Hector J. Ramirez Martinez

The Copernican paradigm shift of the sixteenth century brought about the modern outlook on life that changed the way people viewed the world in the Middle Ages; and introduced a completely new way of understanding humanity. In the same way Western people find we are living now under a radical, new paradigm, a new definition and understanding of what life and humanity are all about. But the interesting thing to consider in this case is that, if in the communist regimes indoctrination and brainwashing took place as an imposition coming overtly and openly from the dictatorship of the ruling party; in the Western countries it has happened, according to the strategies and schemes of the ideologues of the Frankfurt School and its partisans, associates and admirers, in a surreptitious, clandestine and utterly effective way.

What can be called the postmodern paradigm shift has taken place as a conscious, deliberate, and crafty assault like that of a crusade, not with horses and swords by through the much more powerful and subtle force of cultural transformation of the mind, which aimed at destroying the very concept of common sense and humanity itself. This is how Herbert Marcuse, one of the members of the Frankfurt School and probably the most prominent figures of this crusade, describes it in 1967: "The new theory of man also implies the genesis of a new morality as the heir, and the negation of the Judeo-Christian morality." The very morality that had sustained the psychological and ethical convictions and behaviour of western man were the clear target of cultural Marxism and Critical theory, until it finally come plummeting down at the beginning of the twenty first century, under this persistent and ferocious attack.

It certainly was a very clever, crafty, and artful intellectual and cultural strategy; but as Christians we cannot overlook the heavily spiritual aspect of this assault. Though it took place as a merely intellectual, cultural, and psychological transformation it indeed has a very spiritual connotation. In fact, Saul A. Alinsky, an American political and social activist who had some influence in shaping the Western civil rights movement, and author of the book Rules for Radicals, half-jokingly recognized that his struggle for justice and equality was a spiritual one. This is what he says in the introduction of his book: "Lest we forget at least an over-the-shoulder acknowledgment to the very first radical: from all our legends, mythology, and history... the first radical known to man who rebelled against the establishment and did it so effectively that he at least won his own kingdom —Lucifer." And in an interview in 1966 he commented that regarding the hereafter he did not know match but that if it existed, he would choose hell, and that once he got there, he would start organizing it because that is what he really enjoyed in life. "Look out heaven, here we come I´m sure there are lot of grievances that the people down there have and that should be worked out one way or another." And he is not the only one who admits and brags about this attitude, Georg Lukacs, one of the founders of the Frankfurt School expresses himself in the following way: *"Any political movement capable of bringing Bolshevism to the West would have to be Demonic "* and *"The abandonment of the soul's uniqueness solves the problem of 'unleashing' the diabolic forces lurking in all the violence which is needed to create revolution."*

According to J. F. Lyotard in his book The Postmodern

Condition, all the Meta Narratives of Modernism, as he calls them, Christianity, the Enlightenment, Liberalism, even classical Marxism, etc. have been deconstructed and torn down by the postmodern attitude. The actual reality is that following the erosion of Christian values and principles that began during the Enlightenment times, there came the French Revolution, the two World Wars, the Communist Revolution in Russia and China, the permeation of cultural Marxism in the West, the postmodern and applied postmodern attitudes, the globalist political impetus and all the other socio-political and ideological transformation of recent years; and they all have come together to produce, not only the collapse of Christian values, but the very breakdown of reason itself. As disquieting and disturbing as it may sound, this is the devastation state in which the West now finds itself; all objective values have been deconstructed and demolished. And subjective reason has begun to rule rampant everywhere as these ideas have become normalized beliefs that younger people just pick up and adopt as natural and normal, being raised during this pervasive pandemonium.

Thus, with this new paradigm established as the identifying and determining feature of the postmodern Western mind, the twenty-first century human; free from any belief in God, absolutes, or "restrictive" moral values, has as his aim the complete transformation not only of society, social structures, the means of production, and so on but of himself and the natural order. This is how Beatriz Preciado put it in her book Counter Sexual Manifesto: "...you agree to renounce your status as a natural man/woman and you relinquish all privileges that may be extended to you from within the framework of the naturalized heterocentric regime... Counter sexuality is not the creation of a new nature, but rather the end of Nature..."

Alienation, irrationality, and insanity have taken over the West. Douglas Murray author of the book *The Strange Death of Europe* concludes that "Europe has decided to commit suicide." Most people in most countries in the West now feel perfectly justified to advocate, defend, and even impose their own desires and opinions without the need to be based on any form of rational truth or reasonableness, no matter what the issue in question is. And considering that in general terms Western society has accepted a disdain for knowledge, and an approval of apathy toward all means of reasonable discourse; a society has been produced where people feel they have the right to their opinions and ideas, without being questioned about their reasonableness or common sense in any way.

Everyone wants to have the right to say something about everything without having any idea about anything, and their opinions must be taken as set in stone. And this is so because we are no longer dealing with truth or having to make sense; we are living in the new era of post-truth in which it is all about accomplishing one's own aims, personal ambitions, feelings, and desires. Words like tolerance have come to mean that even though someone's ideas may be ill-founded or erroneous, one cannot disagree, let alone try to make the person see the blunder or fallacy in which their argument may be based. As stated by Helen Pluckrose and James Lindsay in their book Cynical Critical Theories, "...Postmodernism rests upon a broad rejection of the correspondence theory of truth: that is, the position that there are objective truths and that they can be established as true by their correspondence with how things actually are in the world. "

We may well say that the twenty-first century is certainly the age of unreason. As in the Feast of Fools at Christmastide in the old days, in which the Lord of Misrule or the Abbot of Unreason would be crowned as the king of the holidays, unreason and misrule have now decidedly and unashamedly taken the stage in our Western societies. The opinion of the scholar, proficient or experienced has the same value as that of the stupid, ignorant, and foolish, and the all-powerful, egotistical, and emotional drive is what determines decisions in most aspects of life and society now.

This might be all very well for a society that does not care about absolutes and truth anymore, but what must be noted is that unless there is some accepted standard of goodness, truth, reasonableness and reality, all society is left with to deal and solve conflicts, concerns and problems are power and control. Your truth, my truth is not somebody else's truth; therefore, socially speaking, there is only the will of one group imposing their ideas on the other and vice versa. And when all this is done in the name of democracy, and all one needs is to get enough social awareness to reach a consensus, so that governments and legislatures take opinions and ideas and turn them into rules, rights, laws and decrees, willpower is endowed with a false legitimacy that will destroy democracy itself.

Willpower is what has created the most horrendous dictatorships in modern and ancient times. When instead of looking at the objective reality of a given situation, whether morally, socially, practically, philosophically, or intellectually speaking; all that counts is the subjective-emotional perception of the other party, the strongest one will overpower the weaker one, and sheer despotic power will rule. And surely and clearly, most of the time, the misuse of power is not going to come from the person ruled by law, ethics, order, and common sense. This is how dictatorships impose their will on most of the population.

Hector J. Ramirez Martinez is associated with *The Ars Vitalis Foundation* in Madrid Spain and has just published his book *Understanding the Times, a Paradigm Shift, and the Arts.*

11

How Not to Respond to Cancel Culture

Akos Balogh

Peter Boghossian was a professor of philosophy at Portland State University, where he taught for ten years. He loved his job. He loved teaching critical thinking to students. And he was committed to questioning everything, including the 'Social Justice' ideology that took over the campus. But his questioning stance led to push-back from students and staff.

The campus authorities investigated him. Students would spit on him as they walked past. And eventually, this became too much for him. So, he quit. In his resignation letter, he wrote: *'While I am grateful for the opportunity to have taught at Portland State for over a decade, it has become clear to me that this institution is no place for people who intend to think freely and explore ideas.'*

Boghossian is another victim of what has come to be known as 'Cancel Culture': the push to marginalise and make life difficult for people who speak up against the prevailing ideology, which in his situation was 'Social Justice Theory'. Or as British researcher Noah Carl puts it, Cancel Culture is '...the practice of pressuring an institution into sanctioning someone because others perceived that they were psychologically or emotionally harmed by something the individual said, or something he did a long time ago.'

Boghossian is raising his voice about the dangers of Cancel Culture and the threat it poses to a free society: The 'chilling effect' on free speech. The conformity it breeds among people afraid of losing their reputations and even their jobs.

And it's a threat many Christians are aware of. We've seen it here in Australia, for example, with the sacking of Rugby Player Israel Folau over an Instagram post about gay people (and others) going to hell without repenting. Or with the Bible Society having to pull a video about Gay Marriage, in the leadup to the 2017 Postal Vote on Same Sex Marriage.

These are real dangers Christians face in our changing culture. But Boghossian sheds light on another danger we face from cancel culture. An overlooked danger, but a threat, nonetheless. And it's a danger Christians should be aware of, lest we succumb to it.

The Overlooked Danger from Cancel Culture

In an interview with podcaster Bari Weiss, Boghossian was asked this question: 'How do you stop yourself from...saying 'if they're not going to play fair, then neither am I... [I will] fight fire with fire?'

In other words, when threatened with cancellation – or when cancelled – how do we stop ourselves from fighting fire with fire? How do we keep from fighting outrage with outrage, hate with hate, cancellation with counter-cancellation?

This is the overlooked danger we face from Cancel Culture. It's not just the cancellation itself (although that's bad, to be sure). Instead, it's our response to Cancel Culture: fighting outrage with outrage.

Now some might say we have a right to play just as dirty. After all, aren't we in a 'culture-war' when it comes to cancel culture? Isn't the future of freedom and Western civilisation at stake? Why shouldn't we respond to outrage with outrage, cancellation with cancellation?

The Danger of Outrage

There are many problems with responding to cancellation with outrage. While it may feel natural, satisfying and even appropriate in the moment, it's dangerous in many ways. God's Word warns us of these dangers:

- It damages others through cruel words that tear people down – people made in the very image and likeness of God. As the book of James points out: 'With the tongue we praise our Lord and Father, and with it we curse human beings, who have been made in God's likeness. Out of the same mouth come praise and cursing. My brothers and sisters, this should not be. (Jas 3:9-10)
- It damages our soul, as we're eaten up with anger toward another: an anger that doesn't achieve the purposes of God (Jas 1:20). But risks escalating and inflaming the situation, making it worse (Jas 3:5-10).
- And it dishonours God, who commands us to show mercy as we've been shown mercy (Matt 18:33). As Jesus commanded us to pray, 'forgive us our sins as we forgive those who sin against us' (Matt 6:12).
- And at worst, it can fuel a cycle of vengeance. It can Balkanise public discourse. And entrench people into hardened positions. Which is one reason why God commands us not to take vengeance into our own hands but leave room for his wrath: 'Do not take revenge, my dear friends, but leave room

for God's wrath, for it is written: "It is mine to avenge; I will repay," says the Lord' (Rom 12:19, 20-21).

The Surprising Benefit of Being Cancelled

But on the other hand, cancellation offers a unique opportunity: an opportunity to show the fruit of the gospel in ways that witness to God's grace.

When we're cancelled and yet respond with grace, we show our world the power of the gospel. Our actions point to the God of forgiveness: the God whose Son prayed for those crucifying him, 'Father forgive them, for they know not what they do' (Luke 23:24). Our mercy points to the God of mercy powerfully and uniquely. Confounding the cynic. And silencing the critic. As the apostle Peter admonished Christians who were facing the threat of being cancelled in a very physical way: 'Live such good lives among the pagans that, though they accuse you of doing wrong, they may see your good deeds and glorify God on the day he visits us.' (1 Peter 2:12). And such 'good deeds' in the context of 1 Peter include the gracious way we treat those that attack us (e.g., 1 Peter 3:9, 4:12-16).

The Impossibility of Forgiveness

But such graciousness and forgiveness doesn't come easy. For most in our culture, it doesn't come at all. The growth of Cancel Culture is a sign that forgiveness and mercy are disappearing, as people shut others down rather than forgiving them.

And forgiveness is disappearing, in large part because in a post-Christian culture we have no way of atoning for our sense of guilt. As essayist William McClay points out in his important essay,

'The Strange Persistence of Guilt', 'The rituals of scapegoating, of public humiliation and shaming, of multiplying morally impermissible utterances and sentiments and punishing them with disproportionate severity, are visibly on the increase in our public life. They are not merely signs of intolerance or incivility, but of a deeper moral disorder, and Unbehagen [disquiet] that cannot be willed away by the psychoanalytic trick of pretending that it does not exist.'

But as Christians, we have a high priest who can sympathise with our weaknesses and atone for our guilt. We can come to him to receive forgiveness and mercy in time of need (Heb 4:16). We don't need to cancel others to feel more righteous about ourselves.

Following The One Who Was Cancelled.

Moreover, we have the example of Christ Himself, in the way he responded to cancellation. He was attacked. The mob piled on. He was cancelled. And yet, he forgave. He entrusted Himself to the One who judges justly (1 Peter 2:23): to the One who promises vengeance (Rom 12:18-21). As Christ was cancelled, he didn't respond with vengeance but with mercy.

The Only Way We'll Forgive

And so, the only sure way that we'll forgive those who cancel us is to remember the One who was cancelled.

If we remember the One who was cancelled for us, if we're overwhelmed by His mercy toward us and the atonement won by his blood, then we'll more likely forgive those who want to cancel us (Matt 18). If we remember the One who didn't repay insult for insult but was gentle toward his accusers, it will impact how we speak. Yes, we should speak the truth to evil. But we should speak with gentleness and respect (1 Peter 3:9, 15).

When facing Outrage and Cancellation, remember the Christ who was cancelled for you. Otherwise, we'll succumb to the temptation of fighting outrage with outrage, cancellation with cancellation.

The Atheist Who Emulates the Way of Christ

Peter Boghossian is an Atheist. But he's a Western Atheist. Which means a cross-shaped culture has profoundly shaped his morality. When asked by podcaster Bari Weiss how he stops himself from hurt the people who hurt him, this is what he said: 'If the question is do I feel tempted to use methods to hurt people, the answer is no. Because to me, this has always been about ideas and not about people. And I harbour no animus against the people who genuinely try to make my life miserable...I really do look at them as victims...of an ideology.'

Here's an Atheist whose gracious response to cancel culture puts many of us Christians to shame. He knows the (overlooked) danger from cancel culture. But he doesn't hurt the people who hurt him because he sees them differently: not as enemies to be destroyed. But, in his case, victims that have been brainwashed.

But as Christians, we have even more reason to beware of the overlooked danger from Cancel Culture. We know how paying back evil with evil dishonours our God. That's how our world might react. But it's not how the servants of the Cancelled King should respond. As He showed mercy to his accusers, so should we. Even to those who cancel us.

References:

[1] Noah Carl, 'Yes, there is such a thing as Cancel Culture', Quillette online, 14 July 2020.

[2] See for example, Akos Balogh, 'Would the beer drinking Christians just shut up!', The Gospel Coalition Australia, 15th March 2017.

[3] Wilfred M. McClay, 'The Strange Persistence of Guilt', *The Hedgehog Review*, Spring 2017 online edition.

Akos Balogh is the former CEO The Gospel Coalition Australia and founder of his blog Akos Balogh.

www.ingramcontent.com/pod-product-compliance
Ingram Content Group UK Ltd.
Pitfield, Milton Keynes, MK11 3LW, UK
UKHW041427180426
11947UKWH00007B/328